FORD N SERIES
TRACTORS

Rod Beemer and Chester Peterson Jr.

Motorbooks International
Publishers & Wholesalers

Dedication

This book is dedicated to our parents, Chester and Erma Peterson Sr., and Lewis and Esther Beemer, who gave us a love for the land. They also provided us with the opportunity to spend countless hours on Ford tractors, undoubtedly appreciated much more now than then.

First published in 1997 by Motorbooks International Publishers & Wholesalers, 729 Prospect Avenue, PO Box 1, Osceola, WI 54020-0001 USA

Motorbooks International books are also available at discounts in bulk quantity for industrial or sales-promotional use. For details write to Special Sales Manager at the Publisher's address

Library of Congress Cataloging-in-Publication Data Available

ISBN 0-7603-0289-8

On the front cover: The red and gray paint scheme for the N Series tractors was adopted when the third generation, the 8N, was introduced in 1947. This tractor is owned by and was restored by Delbert Heusinkveld.

On the frontispiece: Early Model 9Ns had aluminum hoods. They are some of the most collectible Ford tractors.

On the title page: This stunning line-up of Ford tractors belongs to restorer Dwight Emstrom.

On the back cover: **Top:** This restored snowplow is the crowning touch to this Model 8N. **Bottom:** The dash of an aluminum-hooded Model 9N.

Printed in Singapore by PH Productions Pte Ltd

Contents

Introduction

It's always been our belief that books should answer questions, not pose more of them. But as with all beliefs held dear, sometimes adjustments must be made for the real world.

Some of the issues that surfaced during the research for this book must, for the present at least, remain ambiguous. To say there was often a difference of opinion among the collectors and restorers with whom we talked would be a rank understatement. Even among the many printed pages we consulted there were times when nobody agreed on a particular point or issue.

It wasn't a case of anyone being argumentative or hard-headed either. Instead it was perspective, developed by personal experience and/or preference. Some of the specific facts may have been lost over the years too. Or, the definitive answer may still be waiting to be uncovered among the hundreds of thousands of manuscripts and other data in storage at the Henry Ford Museum.

So our effort has been to present conclusions and guidelines based on the best available information we could locate during intensive research for this book's preparation.

Acknowledgments

It takes more than two people to produce a quality book. We'd like to thank these people for unselfishly giving of their time and expertise:

Linda Davis of the Salina Public Library, who chased down the many volumes we requested on Henry Ford, Harry Ferguson, tractor restoration, and other sources of information gleaned for this book.

Dave Mowitz, *Successful Farming* machinery editor, who provided names and addresses that led us to prime "nesting grounds" of collectable Ford tractors—and to some of the nicest people we've ever had the privilege to meet.

Dwight Emstrom, Palmer Fossum, Delbert Huesinkveld, and Johnny and Linda Grist who all endured a writer's many and often "dumb" questions as well as moved scores of their tractors "just a bit" to satisfy the whims of a professional photographer.

The other Ford owners we've pestered, thanks also.

Dan Erikson of Ford Motor Company's still print lab provided archival photos that we needed even when we didn't know what we needed.

Wayne Wolfgram, also of Ford Motor Company, helped us through the maze of photograph releases.

Dr. John Farnworth and John E. Moffitt of the United Kingdom, thank you for your letters and faxes that helped us locate information that otherwise would have been overlooked.

Those many other people who certainly helped our effort, but who didn't know they were doing so, plus anybody we may have overlooked.

And a special thanks to two understanding and long-suffering researching, writing, and photography "widows," Mary Peterson and Dawn Beemer.

The First Ford Tractors

When "Classic Iron" enthusiasts start tossing around phrases such as "changed agriculture forever," "revolutionized the tractor industry," or "changed farming for good and for all time," you know they can only be talking about the Ford N-Series tractors.

Certainly, men such as John Deere, Cyrus McCormick, Daniel Massey, and Jerome Case were persevering, innovative entrepreneurs who excelled in laying the foundation for the development of our modern farm tractors and machinery. But these vibrant personalities pale in comparison to the colorful Henry Ford and the equally brilliant Harry Ferguson.

Garbed in similar battleship gray, the Fordson, the Ford, the Ferguson-Brown, the Ford-Ferguson, and the Ferguson are all part of the family of tractors that revolutionized agriculture. Most people refer to them generically as simply "Ford" tractors or perhaps "Fordson" tractors. (The familiar Ford logo is prominent on the 9N and 2N tractors along with a plate declaring it has the Ferguson System. The Ford emblem alone is featured on the

Left
An experimental Ford V-8 owned by Richard Cummings. When it was donated to the Henry Ford Museum, it was listed as being built in 1937. Before that it was likely the focus of a personal project of Henry Ford's experimental shop at Fair Lane. It was one of several tractors that Ford was working on just before the N-Series tractor was developed. Ford was said to like Allis Chalmers tractors and evaluated several at his experimental farm. And, yes, it appears that the influence of the Allis Chalmers is evident in this design.

Henry Ford, left, and Harry Ferguson, right, discuss the merits of the Ferguson System while a model used to demonstrate the draft control principle sits on the table between them. Ferguson used the spring-powered model tractor to show the advantage of his mounted plow. With the mounted, three-point hitch plow, the tractor stalled. If the tractor pulled a conventional trailing plow, however, the tractor would more likely rear up and possible flip over backward when an obstacle was struck.

8N.) But to collectors, restorers, and old farm boys, it isn't that simple. They know—and appreciate— the sometimes subtle differences.

Who was most responsible for bringing the tractor to the world's farmers? That innocent question could start the revolution all over again

Life and Times of Henry Ford

1847—Grandparents and father migrate from Ireland to the United States as a result of too little food and too much law.

1863 (July 30)—Born at Dearborn, Michigan.

1879—Moves to Detroit and works for Flower Brothers Machine Shop.

1880—Works for Michigan Car Company, a builder of railroad cars.

1882—Returns home to Dearborn, but not to farming.

1884—Attends Goldsmith, Bryant and Stratten Business University in Detroit for three months during the winter of 1884–1885.

1888 (April 11)—Marries Clara Bryant.

1888—Henry and Clara move to Detroit where he works for Detroit Edison Company.

1893—Henry and Clara's first and only child, Edsel, is born.

1896—Builds and drives his first automobile.

1899—Detroit Automobile Company is organized and chartered. Henry quits his job at Edison.

1900—Detroit Automobile Company dissolves.

1901—Organizes Henry Ford Company.

1902—Fired from Henry Ford Company. Company is reorganized as the Cadillac Automobile Company.

1902—Ford and Tom Cooper build two racing cars, "The Arrow" and "999."

1903—Files Ford Motor Company incorporation papers.

1903—Original Model A goes on the market.

1904—Introduces Models B, C, and F.

1905—Expands production plant in Detroit area. Three-hundred workers produce 25 automobiles a day.

1906—Introduces Model N tractor.

1907—Builds his first tractor on Woodward Avenue in Detroit.

1908—Begins to market Model T.

1910—Organizes Henry Ford and Son to further tractor research and design in Dearborn, Michigan.

1914—World War I begins.

1915—Purchases 2,000 acres on the Rouge River.

1916—Builds first experimental Fordson tractor.

1917 (July 27)—Incorporates private company, Henry Ford and Son, Inc., for the express purpose of mass producing the tractor.

1917—Ships a Fordson tractor to British Ford Motor Company.

1917—English government orders first shipment of 5,000 Fordson tractors.

1918—Resigns as president of Ford Motor Company. Son Edsel Ford becomes president.

1918—World War I ends.

1920—Production of Fordson tractors reaches 200,000 for year.

1920—Transfers all Ford family holdings to Ford Motor Company.

1923—Alleged illegitimate son of Henry Ford, John Dahlinger, is born.

1927—Introduces another Model A automobile, this one to become much more famous than the original in 1903.

1927—Shuts down tractor manufacturing due to poor farm economy.

1928—Moves Fordson tractor manufacturing equipment to England.

1938— Makes famous "handshake agreement" with Harry Ferguson.

1939—Beginning of 9N (9 designated the year 1939, N was Ford's designation for tractor) Ford-Ferguson (Ford tractor, Ferguson system) production.

1939—World War II begins in the United Kingdom.

1941—World War II begins in the United States.

1942—2N tractor replaces the new 9N. War rationing brings changes that include steel wheels, no battery and generator, magneto.

1943—Edsel Ford dies; Henry is reinstated as president of Ford Motor Company.

1945—Resigns; Henry II becomes president of Ford Motor Company.

1945—World War II ends.

1946 (December 31)—Ford Motor Company dissolves agreement with Harry Ferguson.

1947 (April 7)—Dies at age 83.

1947 (July 2)—Introduction of 8N Model.

1947—Dearborn Motor Corporation established as marketing firm to replace Harry Ferguson, Ltd.

1948 (January 8)—Harry Ferguson files $341,600,000 lawsuit against Ford Motor Company.

1951—Ferguson vs. Ford suit comes to trial.

1952 (April 9)—Ferguson is awarded $9.25 million.

1953—Model NAA, also known as the Golden Jubilee Model 1903–1953, replaces 8N Model.

depending on which side of the Atlantic you live, to whom you listen, and which books you read.

It's safe to say that Henry Ford and Harry Ferguson were the driving forces behind the tractor. But as with all great achievements, the "name" personalities had help and, in this instance, often lots of help.

For example, when Ford formed Henry Ford & Son in 1915 to develop the Fordson, the predecessor to the N-Series tractor, his 55 percent-owned Ford Motor Company employed more than 14,000 workers. In England, Harry Ferguson had 500 engineers working for him. Although not all worked on the N-Series tractor, many people on both sides of the Atlantic helped work out the details that made the Ford-Ferguson combo the revolutionary achievement it truly was.

Each entrepreneur brought something to the relationship: Ford had the money, production facilities, and vision of a tractor for the small farmer. Ferguson shared his version of that dream and provided the system of implement attachment and his skill as a promoter.

When they got together in 1938 and struck the famous "handshake agreement," they figured they had all their bases covered.

They had money. Ford put in $8 million for tooling and loaned Ferguson $50,000 to help set up the Ferguson marketing program.

They had the dream. Both men had a genuine desire to provide farmers with machines that would lessen the harsh physical labor of farming. Both men also wanted to produce tractors that were more economical to own and maintain than the traditional teams of horses. And both men had the dogged determination of a bulldog on uppers.

They had distribution and promotion. Ford's lieutenant on the tractor project, Charles Sorenson, summed this up with his comment that, "Harry Ferguson could sell you the birds out of the trees."

They had the system. It was Ferguson's. Regardless of later conflicting opinions and allegations from the Ford camp, the patents and the judgment the court awarded Ferguson established the system as Harry Ferguson's invention.

Previously before two problems had plagued the development of a small, low-cost tractor. The first was that of traction, or more properly, a lack of proper traction. It was for this reason that most of the tractor pioneers opted for huge, heavy, exceedingly awkward machines. Second, early tractors employed hitching arrangements that were carried over from horse-drawn implements: Tie them on behind and then draw them

Both Henry Ford and Harry Ferguson used boys and girls to demonstrate the ease of operating their tractor and three-point equipment—which man actually originated the idea is unclear. Regardless, it was most effective in an age where brawn was an important ingredient in farming. In a time when children were considered part of the farm's workforce, the appeal of an eight year old plowing much more with a tractor than an adult could plow with a team of horses must have been decisive in favor of the tractor.

Harry Ferguson demonstrates the Ferguson System at Dearborn, Michigan, in October 1938. Ferguson was a grand showman and his demonstrations were usually planned and arranged with the perfection of a Broadway stage show. His grand finale was roping off a small plot of ground and showing how his tractor, utilizing the three-point Ferguson System, could easily get into the tightest of corners. He further perfected this concept in June 29, 1939, when the new 9N was demonstrated for dealers: A 20x27-foot enclosure was completely plowed without leaving even the faintest of wheel marks.

This 1922 advertisement is aimed at solving the problem of using a tractor with horse-drawn equipment. Farmers already owned horse-drawn equipment and making the change to a "mounted" system meant buying the tractor as well as all new equipment. This appears to be an advance in thinking, cutting the lines to horse farming, over the Rowe design by extending the steering wheel rearward to the implement.

along. The concern was more than a matter of efficiency. For example, if while plowing, the plow caught on an object such as a rock, the horses simply stopped. However, if this occurred with a tractor the engine torque transferred to the rear wheels often caused a small and/or lightweight tractor to rear up and flip-over backward. Because no protective cabs existed in those days, plowing a furrow could, within a split-second, become a life or death situation, especially for tractor operators with less than speedy reflexes.

Harry Ferguson met many farmers who had lost an arm or leg due to a flip-over, while he was working for the English government and attempting to improve the efficiency of tractors. He also encountered numerous widows whose husbands had gone on to that great harvest in the sky due to their unwieldy machines somersaulting backward. This was the catalyst for his revolutionary three-point hitch that—coupled with a hydraulic system and draft control—eventually solved the two problems of traction and flip-overs.

Ferguson and Ford were a great team and the "handshake agreement" was honored until late in 1946, just a few months before Ford passed away in early 1947.

Today, virtually every tractor manufacturer utilizes an evolutionary descendant of the Ferguson System! Is it the single most important

development in mechanical farming? Certainly, it's easy to appreciate an electric starter, rubber tires, or whatever. However, neither they nor any other implementation comes close to the effect of the system Ferguson originated.

The Ford-Ferguson System tractor combo was no flash in the pan either. It's estimated that half of the 884,469 N-Series tractors produced are still in some form of operation around the globe. Many are being used for farming and untold numbers are on "mini-farms," mowing the grass. Others specialize in jobs such as grading lanes and pushing snow.

And, of course, increasing numbers are being restored by collectors who want to ensure that their little piece of history stays alive.

For the record, restoring an N-Series tractor isn't a bad investment. The launch price of the 9N was $585. Yet it's not uncommon for a properly restored N-Series to sell for ten times that amount today.

Look at the back side of this Ford experimental V-8, one of Henry Ford's favorite tractors. Three of this design were built in the mid-1930s; two had a mounted six-cylinder engine while only this one had a V-8 installed. This one-of-a-kind is the only survivor of the trio of higher-powered experimental tractors.

Enough books have been written about Henry Ford to fill a small library. Add those concerning Harry Ferguson and you'd need to buy your book shelves wholesale. Throw in the multitude of books about collecting and restoring tractors and you have more than enough reading to keep you busy for many years.

Just keep in mind that restoring an N-Series tractor is basically a two-step proposition:

1. You first read about the process so you neither spin your wheels nor end up with a non-original-looking result. That's where this book comes in.

2. Then you get some grease under your fingernails and paint on your jeans while doing the actual restoration work that will keep you out of mischief for hours.

Much as we'd like to, we can't be with you in your shop during the lengthy rebuilding and renewal activity. So our objective with this book is to help you by thoroughly illustrating and describing as many of the features—and variations—as we can cram into a single volume.

You don't have to be a restorer to make use of this book either. Maybe you already own a restored N-Series tractor. Or perhaps, as in the case of both authors, you drove one as a child on the farm and learned to appreciate the many attributes of an N-Series tractor at an early age.

In either instance, our intention is to provide you with pertinent information and facts concerning this tractor that truly helped reshape agriculture into its modern format.

Regardless of your interest, you'll have an even deeper appreciation after you learn more about the pair of geniuses that fathered the N-Series. That's why we suggest you read about Henry Ford and Harry Ferguson before you flip the pages to look at the photographs and read the rest of this book. These two men were really larger-than-life giants in their lifetimes.

Henry Ford

Born July 30, 1863, in Michigan, in the dying echoes of the battle of Gettysburg, Henry Ford was the second child of William Ford (1826–1905) and Mary Litogot (1839–1876). Ford's later life was profoundly influenced by the Civil War because he thought he was a reincarnated Civil War soldier.

William Ford's family left Ireland in 1847 when the disastrous potato failure and resulting famine prompted the move to the New World. Two of William's uncles and their family had previously settled in Michigan in 1832.

William eventually became a successful farmer and prominent land owner near present

A 10 to 40% Increase in Your Crop Yield

A seed-bed prepared by the Universal Tiller and the Fordson tractor represents the nearest possible approach to perfection in this first important step. Every inch of the soil is pulverized to the full depth of the plowing; all fertilizer, surface trash or barnyard manure is evenly mixed and distributed; and the result—a gratifying increase in the crop yield, ranging from 10 to 40%, depending on the weather and the condition of the soil.

Nor is this the only advantage gained through the use of the Universal Tiller. One trip over the field with the Tiller and an ideal seedbed is prepared at a great saving of time, money and labor. Go to your Ford dealer today and ask him to arrange for a demonstration. But, in the meantime, send for a copy of our illustrated catalogue giving full information about the Universal Tiller. Write for it today!

UNIVERSAL TILLER

The Universal Tiller Corporation
627 West 43rd Street   New York City

A 1925 ad shows that Ford was progressing toward an implement mounted on the Fordson tractor. The rear wheel was necessary to provide proper depth control, a constant problem that was not overcome until Ferguson perfected his draft control utilizing the three-point hitch. Domestic Fordson production was stopped in 1927; this is probably about as far as the design progressed until the introduction of the Ford-Ferguson 9N tractor in 1939.

Dearborn, Michigan. His son followed his father's footsteps into farming for a few years, although Henry Ford's mechanical interests were to prove a stronger pull.

Something to keep in mind about Henry Ford: He was well into mid-life before he cast off his rather mundane beginnings and series of entrepreneurial failures. The man wasn't an instant success. Regardless, nobody could ever say he wasn't persistent.

Great historical figures gather myth and legend like old tractors gather rust. Some of this may be self-induced, though, and Henry was no exception.

Ford's autobiography, *My Life and Work*, projects the "poor boy makes good" legend of a cruel father, the running away from home to pursue his dream, and his clandestine boyhood watch-repairing episodes.

Ford's sister Margaret, however, recalls no such incidents. Her article, "Memories of My

The controls of Ford's experimental V-8 tractor. Notice the four-spoke steering wheel that is probably the same one used at the beginning of production of the 9N tractor. It is probably also the same steering wheel as the one used on the Ford trucks. One of the company's manufacturing tenets to pare costs was to make as many parts common to more than one model as possible.

Left
This 1922 advertisement shows an aftermarket attachment for the Fordson tractor, the predecessor of the N-Series by almost 15 years. The ad dramatizes the difficulties facing early tractor designers who wanted to mount an implement to the tractor. As the wording in the ad makes quite plain, the company's thrust was that mechanization wasn't really all that different from working with horses. Ford—and other companies— often found the bias for horses and against tractors sometimes almost impossible to overcome. After all, the farmer was the result of generations who had prospered and done well using horses.

Brother, Henry Ford," published in *Michigan History* magazine, must be viewed through the prism of family pride and protectionism of a loved one. Yet her recollections differ significantly on many points concerning her brother's early life on the Ford family farm. The bench and watch repair tools that are now in Ford's room in the restored family home at Greenfield Village, Michigan, were really kept in the parlor, according to his sister. She also recounts that William Ford had the area's best-equipped workshop and that he encouraged Ford's mechanical interests. It was here that Ford spent many hours tinkering with watches and other mechanical devices, no doubt in the company of his father.

Ford's recorded memories of his 1880 departure for employment in the mechanic shops of Detroit is probably more dramatic than absolutely truthful. Instead of running away from home at age 16 to follow his dream against his fathers wishes, it's highly likely that William Ford introduced his son to the Flower brothers. They gave Henry his first mechanic's job in their James Flower and Brothers Machine Shop. The Ford family and the Flower families were friends, and the Flowers were frequent visitors in the Ford home.

Less than a year later, Ford switched jobs to the Detroit Dry Dock Company. However, each fall he went back to the family farm to help with the harvest. After two years, he left Detroit to return to Dearborn and the land.

His developing mechanical prowess was soon demonstrated to the neighbors. This led to employment with the Westinghouse Company, traveling the countryside to service the company's machinery.

In 1886 his father offered Ford 80 acres of timberland in the Dearborn area, which Henry accepted. He cleared the land using a steam road engine.

He married Clara Bryant and had one child, Edsel. Ford built the family's home from timber cut from his land. Then he again returned to

Also used in a Ford truck, the 85-horsepower V-8 in the 1937 Ford experimental tractor burned too much fuel and was too costly to manufacture. It did not meet Henry Ford's requirements for an inexpensive tractor that any farmer could afford. This one-of-a-kind tractor is thought to have been one of Ford's favorites.

Detroit and made several abortive attempts at auto manufacturing.

The key to Henry's eventual success was the Model T. Its popularity generated the wealth that allowed Henry to acquire land and launch production of a tractor. If anybody recalls anything at all about Henry Ford, it's no doubt his remark about the Model T that advised potential buyers, "You can have any color you want—as long as it's black."

All the while, Ford's accomplishments were grabbing the headlines and interest of the American people, Ford was working on his first dream for steam and gasoline power: A tractor to lift the burden of grinding physical labor from those who worked the land. Ford was a farmer first and a mechanic second. The latter was merely a means to make the farmer's work easier and more effective.

It wasn't that Ford disliked farming. Instead, he had an aversion to both the physical labor, which he found exhausting, and the long hours, which took him away from his mechanical interests.

Just ten years after Ford built his first automobile, the quadricyle, he designed his first tractor. By that time his automobile venture was enough of a success to provide the capital and facilities for him to seriously consider tractor development. He

began by assembling a small team to develop the tractor at a facility in Dearborn, Michigan.

That first tractor was, well, a kind of Rube Goldberg affair that relied on Ford's automobile parts wherever possible. However, it worked well enough to further fire Ford's enthusiasm. Unfortunately, the tractor failed to do the same for the shareholders of Ford Motor Company. They were neither happy nor enthused about Ford's fixation with tractors.

Never one to be put off by conflicting opinions of those with whom he worked, Ford immediately formed Henry Ford and Son, Inc., in 1915. All shares of this corporation were held by the Ford family. Ford began to concentrate his efforts on the Fordson tractor at the Dearborn plant.

At this stage of his life, Ford was a folk hero, the Bill Gates or Steve Jobs of his day. The Ford name was frequent front page copy in newspapers all across the United States. More important, his innovative assembly line had made the automobile affordable to the masses.

And, if Henry Ford didn't invent downsizing, he was certainly an early practitioner. At one point, for example, Henry faced the prospect of bankruptcy—he often ignored or put off issues until they had built to crisis proportion. Once faced, however, a crisis was like waving a red cape in

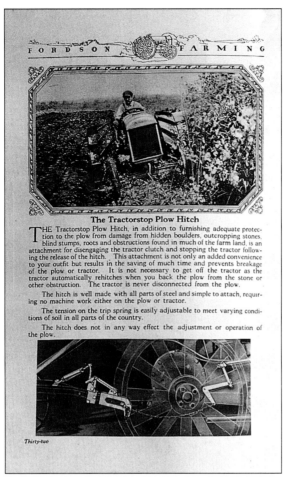

The Tractorstop Plow Hitch

THE Tractorstop Plow Hitch, in addition to furnishing adequate protection to the plow from damage from hidden boulders, outcropping stones, blind stumps, roots and obstructions found in much of the farm land, is an attachment for disengaging the tractor clutch and stopping the tractor following the release of the hitch. This attachment is not only an added convenience to your outfit but results in the saving of much time and prevents breakage of the plow or tractor. It is not necessary to get off the tractor as the tractor automatically rehitches when you back the plow from the stone or other obstruction. The tractor is never disconnected from the plow.

The hitch is well made with all parts of steel and simple to attach, requiring no machine work either on the plow or tractor.

The tension on the trip spring is easily adjustable to meet varying conditions of soil in all parts of the country.

The hitch does not in any way effect the adjustment or operation of the plow.

Thirty-two

This option offered for the Fordson, from the publication Fordson Farming, *addresses the all-too-common problems of rearing up and flipping over when the plow encountered an obstruction. Although this ad does not mention flip-overs, they were serious problems for all designers and manufacturers of early tractors. A handwritten note, "Bought in 1926 by W. A. Grogger, Solomon, Kansas, $476.00," indicates it was in circulation a year before the suspension of Fordson tractor production in 1927.*

front of a bull. In this case, Henry swung into action as only Ford could.

The despised "bureaucracy" at Ford Motor Company was the object of Ford's downsizing. He pared the office staff from 1,074 to 528 people. He eliminated the telegraph office. He merged various vaguely related departments. Then came what looked like the world's largest garage sale. He sold all the now unoccupied desks, typewriters, and filing cabinets. Sixty percent of the telephone extensions also went because, according to Henry, "Only a comparatively few men in any organization need telephones." Finally, he sold all of the company's pencil sharpeners and suggested that any employee wanting to sharpen a pencil should provide his or her own pocketknife!

Ford was also now extremely personally rich. The controversial "$5 a day wage" the company paid to workers had resulted in profits, huge profits. For instance, in 1914 the company stockholders voted themselves dividends totaling $11.2 million.

Ford was also quite forceful. As an example, note that Henry took on the powerful Association of Licensed Automobile Manufactures and won. He managed to get their patent claim on all automobiles thrown out of court. His Highland Park plant provided employment for 14,336 workers. On the downside, all were subjected to the prying eyes and rigid standards of Henry's newly created Sociological Department.

Maybe all of this success made Ford feel he was now invincible, which he learned he really wasn't when he launched an endeavor that wouldn't yield to his genius and riches. Ford believed in reincarnation—and that in a previous life he had been a Civil War soldier slain in battle. He was also an avowed pacifist at a time when the United States was being drawn into the World War I conflict and patriotic feelings were running high. This combination of beliefs made Ford decide to use his mind and vast wealth to bring peace to the world. Surely, he reasoned, if the leaders of the opposing nations sat down and talked, and Henry was there, peace could be achieved. His idea: A hastily conceived plan know as the Peace Ship involved chartering a ship to take diplomats and leaders to a special conference.

Conflicting personalities doomed the scheme from the start, though. The result was Ford's biggest defeat to date, plus some extremely negative publicity. Those involved in the plan continued to work on it in Europe for a year at Ford's expense with no real results except for the tab of a half-million dollars. Eventually the U.S. press flip-flopped and turned more kindly toward Ford's efforts. Editorials pointed out that at least he had made an effort to preserve world peace and that he had certainly put his money where his mouth was.

Don't worry about Ford's financial situation, though. He got his money back, and more, after he shoved aside his pacifist ideals and decided to help end the war by doing what he did best: Mass producing machinery and equipment, in this case military products. His Highland Park plant produced tanks, airplanes, steel helmets, ammunition boxes, armor plating, airplane engines, and gas masks. Ford even proposed a small, one-person submarine that featured a "pill on a pole." This was a pole with a bomb on the end that could be planted on an enemy battleship as the submarine ran beneath it.

To justify his switch from pacifism to war production, Ford vowed he would return his share of all profits from the company's arms production to the

Life and Times of Harry Ferguson

1884 (November 4)—Born in the tiny village of Growell, Northern Ireland; christened Henry George. Parents James and Mary.

1902—Works in Belfast with brother in machine shop; displays remarkable talent for tuning engines.

1904—Starts riding motorcycles to publicize his brother's business.

1908—Becomes interested in aviation and builds his own airplane five years after the first flight of the Wright Brothers.

1910—Makes first successful three-mile flight in Ireland.

1911—Starts his own motor business on May Street in Belfast.

1912—Changes name of company to Harry Ferguson, Ltd.

1912—Company is agency for Vauxhall automobiles and Waterloo Boy tractors. Takes up auto racing.

1913—Marries Maureen Watson, with whom he later has one daughter, Betty.

1914—Begins running guns for the Ulster Volunteer Force—an anti-Catholic organization.

1917—Irish Board of Agriculture asks Ferguson to improve efficiency of Ireland's tractors.

1917—Begins design for a better plow. Decides to fit it to the Ford Eros tractor, itself a conversion of the Model T car.

1917—On learning of the possibility of the Fordson tractor being built in Great Britain, takes his plow drawings to London to meet with Ford representative Charles Sorenson. Sorenson encourages further work on the design.

1917—Completes his first Ferguson plow for the Eros. However, it's immediately outdated due to the introduction of the Fordson to Great Britain and the announcement that 5,000 Fordsons are to be imported from the United States. Modifies the inventory of Eros plows for use with the Fordson. Sells them and develops a plow with a duplex hitch for the Fordson, for which he obtains a patent.

1920—Demonstrates plow to Henry Ford at the Rouge plant in Michigan. Because no steel casting facilities exist in Belfast, the plow has bronze beams. Ford is impressed, but misjudges Ferguson by offering him a job with Ford. Ferguson refuses. Ford offers to buy the patent rights. Ferguson refuses. The men part leaving the door open for future contact.

1925—Files for draft control patent in Great Britain and the United States. Granted in June 1926.

1925—Establishes Ferguson-Sherman, Inc., to manufacture plows. Sherman is an American investor whose company manufactures farm implements and parts.

1927—Fordson tractor production ceases in the United States.

1936—Ferguson-Brown tractors start production. Brown's family owns the biggest gear manufacturing factory in England and Brown invests. The tractor is all-black in color.

1938—Eber Sherman, the "Sherman" of Ferguson-Sherman, Inc., witnesses demonstration of Ferguson-Brown tractor in England. Returns to the United States to tell Henry Ford about its merits. Ford asks if Ferguson would come to Dearborn to again demonstrate his newer system. Ferguson ships tractor number 722 and a set of implements to the United States.

1938—Demonstration of Ferguson system at Dearborn results in famous "handshake agreement."

1939—Ferguson and David Brown dissolve partnership.

1939—Field-tests first prototype of Ford-Ferguson tractor.

1939—David Brown introduces his own tractor that utilizes a hydraulic lift.

1941—Eber Sherman resigns from Ferguson-Sherman, Inc. Name changes to Harry Ferguson, Inc.

1942—War rationing temporarily closes production at Ford's Rouge tractor plant. Management launches a drive to have Ferguson distributors and dealers locate old Fordson tractors so they can be shipped to Ford plant to be broken up and re-smelted for production of new Ford-Fergusons. Copper is in short supply so Ford engineers produce a version with no electric starter motor; they also produce some tractors with steel wheels instead of rubber tires.

Meanwhile, Ferguson goes straight to the top and persuades President Franklin Roosevelt to see a demonstration of the Ford-Ferguson tractor. Roosevelt buys a Ford-Ferguson tractor and range of implements for his Hyde Park, New York, farm. He ensures material for the resumption of manufacturing. Modified tractor becomes Model 2N.

1946—First TE 20 model tractor comes off production line in England. It's an almost exact copy of Dearborn Ford, but with a four-speed transmission.

1946—Effective June 1947, Ford discontinues agreement with Harry Ferguson to produce tractors.

1946—Ford Motor Company establishes Dearborn Motor Corporation as a replacement marketing company for Harry Ferguson, Inc.

1947—Introduction of Ford 8N with unchanged Ferguson system of hydraulics and linkage along with 22 new modifications, biggest of which is a four-speed transmission.

1948—Ferguson files two lawsuits that total $341 million, plus "reasonable attorney fees and costs," against Ford.

1948—First U. S.-built Ferguson tractors roll off line in Detroit.

1949—Ferguson's Coventry, England-built tractor has 78 percent of market in Great Britain.

1950—Establishes a new company, Harry Ferguson Research.

1953—Canadian-based Massey-Harris and Harry Ferguson, Ltd. merge. Ferguson receives 1,805,055 shares valued at $16 million.

1953—Churchill proposes knighthood for Ferguson who refuses the honor.

1954—Sells his shares of Massey-Harris-Ferguson to Massey-Harris.

1958—Re-enters tractor development.

1960—Develops Formula 1 racing automobile called Project 99.

1960—Dies of barbiturate overdose at age 76—it's never established whether his death was accidental or intentional.

The 1937 V-8 Ford experimental tractor borrowed heavily from the other products on the line at Ford Motor Company. The side lift hood, for example, is pretty much vintage Ford truck.

government. So far, however, no records have been found that indicate Ford ever repaid the government one penny of the estimated $29 million that his 58.5 percent share of the company reaped.

In 1919 Ford bought out all the minority stockholders of Ford Motor Company. He then consolidated ownership totally in the Ford family: Fifty-five percent in his name, 42 percent in son Edsel's name and the remaining three percent in wife Clara's name. The following year he merged Henry Ford & Son Company into the Ford Motor Company.

The Fordson was a good tractor for its time. It held its own against other, often larger tractors. Being both small and inexpensive helped it sell well despite some problems it shared with other makes. These problems included lack of weight, which allowed wheel slippage in some conditions, and the nasty habit of rearing over backward if the plow encountered an obstruction. Even at this primitive stage, and with all its faults, the age of tractor power established a firm foothold on U.S. farms.

Good news: By 1925 Ford had already built its 500,000th Fordson tractor!

Bad news: The combination of severe economic recession and plummeting farm income depressed the market. So in 1927 Ford Motor

Company closed down its U.S. tractor production. Production continued in England, however.

For the next ten years the U.S. Ford tractor division was dormant except for work on some experimental models. Much of this work was done in a building close to Ford's palatial home, Fair Lane.

In the meantime, Ford also went into the airplane business, and in a big way. In 1924 Fordson tractors started leveling 260 acres beside the new engineering laboratories in Dearborn, Michigan. Hangers were built and runways constructed. Tons of crushed white stone were positioned so that the word "FORD" was large enough to be seen by an aviator two miles up in the sky.

In the next nine years, Ford pioneered the United States' first regularly scheduled passenger flights, between Cleveland and Detroit; the first air-mail service; and the first use of radio to guide a commercial airliner. He also manufactured a William B. Stout design that became known as the Ford Tri-Motor. It was the first all-metal, multi-engine airplane. The Great Depression served Ford notice, though, that it was time for him to concentrate his efforts on making cars and cease aircraft production.

In 1937, reports filtered back to Ford from England that Harry Ferguson had developed an

Richard Cummings, Rochester Hills, Minnesota, purchased and restored 1937 Ford experimental tractor at auction from the Henry Ford Museum in 1982. The tractor had been donated to the museum 30 years earlier and had been displayed for several years. Then, for some unknown reason, it was moved outside from 1958 to 1982 where it deteriorated badly.

impressive tractor and hitch design. Ford was interested and invited Ferguson to demonstrate his concept at Fair Lane. This was precisely what Harry Ferguson wanted to hear. He shipped a tractor and set of implements to the United States. The eventual result was the development of the N-Series tractor.

As they say, the rest is history—not to mention perhaps the most important industrial development in agriculture.

Harry Ferguson

From the viewpoint of those in the Ford camp, Ferguson was a foreign opportunist who rode to riches on Ford's shirttail after the famous "handshake agreement" of 1938 launched the N-Series in 1939.

For example, Charles Sorenson was Ford's production man who did much to get the Ford tractor plant into high gear. His book, *My Forty Years with Ford*, portrays Ferguson as being limited in ability to design and essentially a poor man looking for a job. However, the book was later withdrawn from all British book shops. Ferguson obtained an apology and was awarded costs by the High Court.

Harry Ferguson was neither a poor man nor jobless when he shook hands with Henry Ford. To

The headlights were originally Ford truck production line items but were missing when the restorer purchased the tractor. Unable to find the exact truck headlights, the restorer installed Model A headlights until the correct lights can be located. Other stock Ford items include an 85-horsepower V-8 engine, four-speed transmission from a 1937 truck, grill and radiator from a 1935 truck, Ford car wheels on tricycle front end, and rear wheels the same as the English Ford and Allis Chalmers tractors.

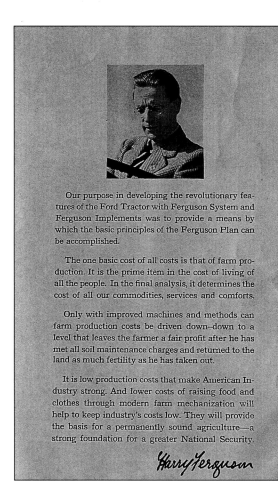

Our purpose in developing the revolutionary features of the Ford Tractor with Ferguson System and Ferguson Implements was to provide a means by which the basic principles of the Ferguson Plan can be accomplished.

The one basic cost of all costs is that of farm production. It is the prime item in the cost of living of all the people. In the final analysis, it determines the cost of all our commodities, services and comforts.

Only with improved machines and methods can farm production costs be driven down—down to a level that leaves the farmer a fair profit after he has met all soil maintenance charges and returned to the land as much fertility as he has taken out.

It is low production costs that make American Industry strong. And lower costs of raising food and clothes through modern farm mechanization will help to keep industry's costs low. They will provide the basis for a permanently sound agriculture—a strong foundation for a greater National Security.

Harry Ferguson

An interesting page from a Harry Ferguson publication sets forth his policy and beliefs on farm equipment and agriculture.

say that Ferguson lived an interesting life would be as much an understatement as simply commenting that Babe Ruth was a pretty fair baseball player.

The Lawsuit

Maybe it would be better to call it THE lawsuit, one of the most famous in history and certainly in agriculture.

As long as Henry Ford was alive the "handshake agreement" worked. There never was one word of any sort written on paper. The agreement was a case of two strong personalities, each of which firmly held the reins of his company, agreeing man-to-man.

However, a post World War II cost analysis showed that the Ford tractor division had lost approximately $25 million during World War II. So, Ford Motor Company dissolved its oral agreement with Ferguson and launched its own 8N tractor in 1947, using Ferguson's patents. Understandably, Harry Ferguson took exception, filing two lawsuits totaling $341 million worth of exception to be more precise.

The media then was mostly flashbulbs, note-pads, typewriters, telexes, and movie house newsreels. Nevertheless, the lack of modern TV coverage did not prevent the Ferguson-Ford trial from racking up some impressive legal milestones, perhaps rivaling the O. J. Simpson trial of almost a half-century later.

By the time a settlement was reached, Ferguson had sat through 30 days on the stand. He answered over 60,000 questions that filled 11,000 pages of verbatim reports. A Ferguson employee by the name of D'Angelo set the witness stand record, though, at 40 days of testimony.

Henry Ford II, Henry Ford's grandson, also spent upward of 30 days on the stand. One witness committed suicide by jumping from his fourteenth floor hotel window.

The entire litigation involved more than 80,000 depositions, in excess of a million documents, and 200 lawyers. It cost Ferguson approximately $3.5 million.

Before the court could reach a verdict, however, Ferguson decided to settle out of court. This settlement awarded Ferguson $9.25 million, representing patent royalties and the withdrawal of all claims, including Ford's counterclaim.

Both sides claimed victory.

Almost Enough Similarities To Be Twins

How and why did the "handshake agreement" last as long as it did?

It's said that in later years Ford and Ferguson looked enough alike to be brothers—which you can judge for yourself from the photographs. It's thought that the agreement was successful for so long because these two pace-setting men had so much in common and ruled their own company as their fiefdom. Other similarities include the following:

• Both were Irish. Ford's family originally came from Ireland, while Ferguson was born in Ireland.

• Both had the first name of Henry, although Ferguson always went by the name of Harry.

• Both fathered one child.

• Both were raised in rural areas, close to the land and farming.

• Both were intuitive.

• Both were called mechanical genius.

• Both were dedicated to adapting tractor power to farming.

• Both were tenacious in pursuing their dreams.

• Both could be devious when the situation required it. For example, Ford forced his minority stockholders to sell by moving to California and then announcing he was working on a new automobile, a better and cheaper car that would be in direct com-

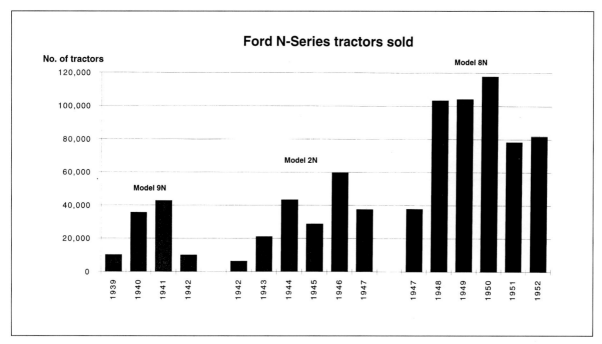

Ford N-Series tractors sold

No. of tractors

Model 8N

Model 2N

Model 9N

This bar graph makes it easy to see the production numbers of the N tractor. The war's impact is dramatic and 1951 and 1952 numbers show a significant drop. It's thought that this decrease in production was due to the demand by farmers for bigger, more powerful tractors.

petition with the Model T. As soon as he had control of Ford Motor Company again, the idea was dropped.

Harry Ferguson lied to his partner David Brown about his 1939 visit to Henry Ford. When David Brown went ahead with some design changes on the Ferguson tractor without Ferguson's approval, Ferguson terminated the relationship. This effectively cut Brown out of any profits from the later Ford-Ferguson success.

•Both men were dictatorial in their dealings with employees. The touted "Ford $5 dollar a day wage" was really $2.64 in wages and $2.36 "profit sharing." Ford viewed this sharing of profit as his right to supervise how those profits were spent. He instituted the Ford Motor Company's Sociological Department whose responsibilities included dispatching teams of men to inspect the homes and personal living habits of employees.

Harry Ferguson was intolerant of personal dress that in any way differed from his own standards. He straightened ties of employees and instructed them on how to fold their lapel hand-

kerchiefs. Smoking and drinking were no-nos—except for Ferguson's wine and cigars, that is. Anyone who disagreed with Ferguson did not work for him long.

Despite these attitudes, both men enjoyed a high degree of loyalty among top employees—at least until the employees were no longer deemed necessary by Ford or Ferguson.

•Both men rejected standard religion. Ford embraced reincarnation. Harry was an atheist.

•Both men raced automobiles and liked all nines in their car numbers: "999" for Ford and "99" for Ferguson.

•Both men became involved in aviation.

•Both men, early in their careers attended an institution of higher learning: Ford the Goldsmith, Bryant and Stratten Business University in Detroit and Ferguson the Belfast Technical College.

•Both men apparently had great difficulty in reading blueprints.

•Both men seemed to have an aversion to horses, almost a hatred, in fact.

Two

The Model 9N

Henry Ford's desire to build tractors to lessen the hard labor of farming didn't stop in 1927 when he withdrew the Fordson from U.S. production. Fordson tractors continued to be built in Cork, Ireland, and also later in Dagenham, Essex, England. In the United States, the Sherman brothers were a leading importer of the English-built Fordson.

In the United States, however, the "dream" suffered through a decade of inactivity—except for the experimental tractors that were still being developed in a small building close to Ford's Fair Lane home.

Fordson sales numbered in the hundreds of thousands worldwide. But perhaps the problems that had beset Ford's domestic tractor division was the reason Henry let it languish so long at home. While it no doubt seemed logical at the time to company executives, the marketing strategy for the Fordson tractor was ill-conceived at charitable best. That's because the decision was made to market the tractors through the company's already established auto dealerships.

On the surface, of course, this wasn't a bad idea. That is, it wasn't until you stop to consider that a dealership in downtown New York City probably didn't have a really large clientele in immediate need of tractors. Nor did the dealerships in moun-

This engine on the earliest-known production 9N, Serial Number 16 (and so the earliest Ford-Ferguson tractor on which records are available) shows several early variations from later production models. Notice that the crankcase breather pipe is located farther to the rear than is found on later tractors. Also, the oil filter is back almost where the toolbox was finally mounted on later production 9Ns. And it's equipped with a four-blade push fan, which was later replaced with a pull-type fan to alleviate engine overheating in tough working conditions. The serial number location is at the far rear left of the block.

Left
9N Serial Number 16 is, as far as is documented, the earliest N-Series tractor still in existence in the world. Those familiar with the Ford tractor factory believe it came off the production line no later than the second day, and possibly as early as the first day that the assembly line was fired up.

Compare this cast-aluminum steering column on 9N Serial Number 16 with later production tractors. Yes, the difference is immediately apparent. There's no identification plate on the top of the casting, but it has a casting number of 70.

tainous regions or areas with little or no cultivated farm ground. Many such dealerships simply weren't prepared to sell the Fordson tractor, much less provide service or advice, because they barely knew a drawbar from a cornstalk. The Ford auto dealerships weren't deliriously happy about the situation.

Adding another concern atop an existing problem, Ford at the time was also locked in a bitter trade war with International Harvester and General Motors. This strife lasted for ten long years. During this time, Ford pared the price of its Fordson tractor from $750 to just $395. To compensate for this much lower price, the company had to cost-cut and strive for larger volume production.

Railcar after railcar of tractors rolled out of Dearborn and descended on unsuspecting dealerships irrespective of the dealers' needs or wishes. Arriving tractors had to be paid for with hard cash too. This often left dealers cash poor, not to mention swamped with a product they couldn't sell at a profit.

It didn't help dealers that paying with cash on arrival was an established practice of the Ford company with automobiles as well. If the factory needed cash flow, well, just ship unrequested cars and unrequested parts. To be fair, Ford wasn't alone in this practice during this period of automotive history. Most other auto manufactures operated in like fashion. Regardless, the practice moved some auto dealerships into a "high risk" category in the 1920s and

1930s and was responsible for forcing a wave of failed dealerships, including many Ford dealerships.

International Harvester, on the other hand, was the expert in agriculture equipment production and marketing. The company spent millions and then more millions challenging Ford and General Motors for leadership in placing tractors and agricultural machinery on the nation's farms.

General Motors capitulated early, though. By 1922 it had taken its tractor, the Samson, out of the competition. This later world leader in the automobile business seemed satisfied to acknowledge its defeat and lick its wounds—an estimated $33 million loss—and focus on auto production instead.

Ford, however, struggled on for a few more innings of a game that was already lost to harder-hitting International Harvester. The Fordson just

The dash arrangement on early 9Ns and the four-spoke steering wheel with the chrome center. Notice the location of the ammeter gauge, switch key, starter button, and ignition light on this tractor.

wasn't enough tractor for the large farming operations that were then opening up in the United States' western farming country and which demanded more horsepower. Finally, in 1927, the Fordson went the way of the Samson.

Yet another problem, on top of all the others, was the touchy one that made marketing difficult for Fordson sales personnel. This was the occasionally unfortunate desire of the tractor to emulate a spooked horse and rear up on it rear wheels. On hilly ground or rocky soil the Fordson demonstrated this nasty habit with such regularity that one farm magazine suggested, not all in jest, that the tractor come complete from the factory with a red-lettered decal warning, "Prepare to meet thy God." In 1922 *Pipp's Weekly* ran a list of 136 Fordson drivers who had been either killed or injured while operating the tractor.

With this background in mind, it's easy to understand why Henry Ford reportedly announced, "This is it!" after witnessing the Ferguson demonstration of the three-point hitch on its Ferguson-Brown tractor.

Getting in harness with Ferguson—with one simple handshake—was the solution to many problems. The mounted implements solved the rearing problem. And Henry Ford figured Harry Ferguson's organizational and sales prowess would solve the marketing dilemma without antagonizing the already tractor-weary Ford auto dealerships. Henry Ford was back in the tractor business again.

Henry wasn't one to dally once his mind was made up. The famous handshake agreement in 1938 was followed by feverish activity at the Rouge River plant. Charles Sorenson, chief of production, was given a free hand to expedite the enormous tooling job of getting production of the tractor up and running.

Sorenson wasn't one known to dally either. His hard-driving style of management motivated employees to peak output. The design was approved in October 1939 and production soon began on the first model, the 9N. It was almost ten years later that the final design was stabilized in the 8N model, after modifications and improvements appeared in both the 9N and the 2N that followed.

As with all new products, the design was subject to occasional "It'd be better if..." changes. Some of these modifications came from the drawing board, some from later field tests, and some were event-driven. With the N-Series, some no doubt came from the intuitive Henry and Harry themselves.

Not as much has been written about Ford's tractor production as about the manufacture of the company's automobiles. But it's reasonable to

A rare feature—the left lift link is threaded on the bottom of this 9N, manufactured at near the beginning of the production run.

assume that what worked so well for the Model T and other Ford autos was assuredly carried over to the tractor factory. Ford's comment, "The company can never hope to make a go of large-scale production until all its products are made as much alike as pins or matches," no doubt also prevailed at the tractor production facilities. This statement, uttered some time before 1908, gives a good indication of Ford's philosophy concerning manufacturing. It would have some bearing on the relatively few major variants of the Model N Ford tractors too.

Considering how quickly the tractor went into production, it's a tribute to its designers and engineers that so few big changes were eventually required.

Although this isn't a book about engine building, several interesting facts about the 9N's engine focuses some light on the manufacturing genius of Henry Ford.

The four-cylinder "L" flathead engine was really half of the automobile V-8 engine the company was producing during this period. Certainly this made for less expensive manufacturing costs and aided the bottom line.

"Cast and chromed" aptly describes the early 9N radiator cap. The distinctive art deco styling remained the same throughout all N-Series production. The finish and method of manufacture, however, changed twice in subsequent production.

There are two items I recall reading in the *Newsletter* that prompt me to write. The first concerns someone's comment about the spanner sent out with the 9N, implying, I think, that this was the idea of Henry Ford. In fact, the spanner is identical, apart from the logo, to the Ferguson tractor spanner issued before the war from 1936 to 1939 with the Ferguson A.

I have two of these spanners. One is still on the tractor supplied to a member of my family when purchased new. This seems to suggest that the idea of supplying a wrench with a new tractor was brought into the process by Harry Ferguson.

The second point is an item in the Winter 1991 issue concerning parts for

The crossover of production parts wasn't limited to the "L" head. It was a major cost saving in tooling too. By designing and building with parts already in the production stream, automobile and tractors parts could be interchanged. For example, the timing gears, intake valves, and other internal engine parts all came out of the same parts bin as the company's Mercury V-8 engine. Starters from the Ford small V-8 and the 9N tractor were the same. Large Ford trucks and the 9N shared the same rear axle rings and pinion gears.

The 9N was much more similar in appearance to the Ferguson-Brown tractor than it was to the Fordson or most of the experimental tractors that Ford was working on at the time. Although approximately 10 percent larger than the Ferguson-Brown tractor used in the famous demonstration by Ferguson, there were resemblances between the two.

As the old saying notes, "What goes around, comes around." Because, in this case, that Ferguson-Brown showed numerous similarities to the Fordson built by Ford that was prevalent in England before Ferguson built his own first tractor.

Just how much of the final design was Ford's and how much was Ferguson's will probably never be established. Certainly few of the experts agree about the contributions of both partners. Of course, if you own an N tractor it doesn't matter as long as your tractor works and looks good enough to suit you. But to those with a historical or archival bent, it's a controversial topic. Any conclusion will, in final draft, reflect which side of the big pond you live on.

George Fields, chief executive officer of The Ferguson Club and Journal, wrote this letter in the *9N-2N-8N-NAA Newsletter* (volume 7 number 1, Winter, 1992):

Take a good look at this cast-aluminum grill that looks just like the original equipment on the first production run of 9N tractors. This isn't an original grill, however, although it conforms quite closely to original Ford specs.

When the horizontal bars were replaced with vertical rods, the center rib remained solid as it was on the horizontal bar grill. This original 1941 9N tractor is missing the Ford emblem. Otherwise, it exhibits Ford factory originality.

Fergusons. I have interviewed some of the people who were in Detroit at the time and some who did design work in England in the run-up to making the TE tractors in England.

It seems the "handshake" deal between Harry Ferguson and Henry Ford continued a Ferguson policy from which Ferguson rarely varied: Retaining his own total control over design.

Having read the patents from the 1920s and 1930s, it is my opinion that there is virtually nothing in principle in the 9N tractor that was not covered by one of the patents granted to Harry Ferguson.

He presented Henry Ford with a blueprint of his designs for the new Ferguson tractor in late 1938. This was the replacement of the Ferguson "A" that had been used in the famous demonstration at Fair Lane.

These documents have not come to light, but it is rumored that Henry Ford II, after

his father's death, destroyed them. I elaborated on this with my comments on Patent 510,352 in last winter's *Ferguson Club Journal*.

As for the detailed working drawings used in the production of the 9N, these were probably drawn by personnel from both companies, but always under Ferguson's eagle eye and, in aspects of principle, always conforming to Ferguson's patents and requirements.

One of the accepted facts of manufacturing both yesterday and today is the practice of getting your hands on the competition's products. The products can then be tested, measured, weighed, and probed. Those parts or designs you like can be, well, copied. Patents sometimes dictated that only a small change be made to circumvent its coverage.

For example, the initial step Ford engineers took with the prototype Ferguson-Brown was to completely dismantle it. Of first concern was the hydraulic system and the draft control. No doubt other worthy features also found their way into the new N-Series tractor. That's progress.

Model 9N Variations

Once you've decided that what you have or what you want is the 9N Ford-Ferguson, you'll want to know what's special about your tractor or how it may differ from other 9Ns. Some of the early variants featured on these tractors make them highly collectable. Suggestion: It's to your benefit to keep your tractor in as original condition as possible.

What usually comes to mind about the early 9Ns are the model's cast-aluminum hoods, grill, and side panels. The original first production 9N grills were chromed cast-aluminum. Finding an original of either can be as exciting as winning the lottery. And buying one may verge on being as expensive as paying off a winning lottery number.

As the story goes, the stamping machines for the steel metal hoods weren't ready to come online when production started. So, Charles Sorenson, had his son, who was in the foundry business, cast the hoods out of aluminum.

These original hoods came painted gray like the rest of the metal work. Unfortunately, the aluminum proved susceptible to breakage and Ford was later forced to issue a recall. An owner could exchange his original aluminum metal work for the new steel components.

Restorers today are leaving these aluminum hoods unpainted and polishing them to a high luster. This results in a tractor of striking appearance that quickly earns attention from even non-Ford admirers.

How many 9Ns were launched with aluminum cast hoods? The numbers you'll hear most

A sight to make the heart pound mightily in the chest of any dedicated Ford tractor restorer's chest: an all-original 1941 9N. To the uninitiated, it looks like a junker. But to those restorers with vision, this tractor represents the potential to produce a show-stopping classic.

often are 600 to 700. But a letter published in the Summer 1987 issue of the *N Newsletter* seems to substantiate that as many as 3,105 left the factory this way. A possible explanation is that when the cast hoods were replaced with steel hoods, other parts on the tractor were still cast-aluminum. This includes the grill with horizontal bars, the dash and steering housing, the hydraulic control lever quadrant, and transmission housing inspection covers.

Nobody knows how many aluminum hoods have survived, because they were so subject to stress fractures and other problems that many owners replaced them with steel hoods. But if you're lucky enough to locate one, even a hood in need of extensive repair, it's well worth your investment.

The original aluminum hood's battery cover is attached to the hood with clips. As the years went by these were subject to breakage. Many were fit-

ted with various handmade devices to keep the cover in place. The original clips are held in place by two rivets on the front clip. The clips are one piece, side-to-side. The back clip has three original rivets. Many of the repaired units have an extra hole or two drilled for rivets or bolts. Once the aluminum hoods were replaced with steel hoods, the same style battery cover and clips were used until 1940.

The original cast-aluminum grills just didn't survive. The semi-horizontal bars weren't much more than 1/4-inch thick. A slap of a cornstalk or tall weed was often enough to break these fragile bars. Bits and parts of these grills are around, although it doesn't appear that more than a handful survived intact. Today, aftermarket grills are available. A good reproduction would be desirable if your original tractor came with the aluminum grill and you have an aluminum hood and side panels.

A small but integral part of the three-point hitch, the spring-loaded linch-pin was patented by Harry Ferguson. Although today it's probably one of the most common items around almost any machine shed, it's seldom given much thought—except when you can't find one when hooking up a piece of equipment in order to head for the field.

The original aluminum grills had three bars below the crank hole. After Ford switched to steel grills, there are four bars below the crank hole. This ID point can serve only as a general rule, though, because photographs taken of the first 9Ns during development and of experimental models are not consistent. Some photographs show grills with as many as five bars below the crank hole while other grills have as few as two. A good guess is that the foundry had more than one casting pattern available. Remember, of course, that this tractor was developed and put on the market in an extremely short span of time.

Aluminum side panels—also referred to as hood legs—suffered the same fate as the grills. Cast-aluminum reproductions are available,

although they will probably require patience to custom fit to match your tractor. Most come without any attachment hole so they can be drilled to match your tractor.

Some subtle variants of the early 9Ns are worth noting. On the 9N Serial Number 16, the oil fill or crankcase breather tube is located back from the front of the block approximately 2 to 3 inches. Again, this seems to be the only exception from the extreme front location on the block until the 8N model arrived.

Also on 9N Serial Number 16, the left stabilizer bar on the three-point hitch is threaded on both ends. The reason for this isn't known, and nobody has ventured a guess. Or, as one Ford tractor owner comments, "I don't know, and if I say anything I'd be lying, and once I start I can't quit." Incidentally, this is typical of most Ford tractor restorers, both amateur and professional. They'll generally admit they don't know something rather than attempting to impress you with a guess.

Production of the 9N started off the line with a four-blade radiator fan pitched to push the air forward through the radiator cores. Its purpose was to keep the heat of the engine away from the operator. It didn't prove all that successful, however, because it instead picked up the engine heat and blew it across the radiator cores. This severely limited the efficiency of the cooling system. Engine overheating often was the result of working under high heat conditions and/or pulling a heavy load.

A 9N that displays a manifold with long throat to carburetor. These early manifolds weren't as wide across as manifolds on later tractors. It's thought that perhaps the narrow style manifold didn't allow enough exhaust flow.

Later production reversed the air flow. These fan blades are pitched to instead pull the air through the radiator. But the push-bladed fan continued to be offered in some parts catalogs. The *Ford-Ferguson Accessories Booklet* circa 1939 or 1940 lists both types. It states that in high grass or other dusty conditions the push-type fan keeps the radiator cores cleaner. Ford N tractors can have either a push- or pull-fan in either a four- or six-blade design.

Beginning production (1939 through 1941) included different formats on the instrument panel. In 1939, the switch key is on the right and the starter button located at the left. The dash had three different arrangements in the 1940 model year alone. First the starter button was on the dash's left side with the key on the right side. Next the starter button was moved to the transmission with the key remaining on the right side. Then the key was again moved to the lower left side of the instrument panel. In 1941, the key switch was yet again repositioned, this time to the left side of the steering column. The starter button remained on the transmission cover.

If you're striving for total originality, a small but important detail concerns the wrenches that originally were supplied with the tractor. They're a handy, thoughtful touch. The Ford-New Holland parts catalog lists four wrenches 1939–1952: Wrench, Open End, 11/16 inch–1 inch; Wrench, Open End, 11/16 inch–1 1/16 inch; Wrench, Open End, 9/16 inch–5/8 inch, and Wrench, Adjustable. This assortment of wrenches allows the operator to make in-the-field adjustments or repairs of minor nature.

An innovative and handy idea was the marking on the handle of one wrench that also served as a sort of gas gauge: Dip the wrench into the gas tank, then refer to the markings to see how much fuel you have left. Incidentally, there's no worry about dropping this wrench into the gas tank. That's because the wrench's large open end is too large to fit through the gas filler opening. You can also use this handy wrench to measure furrow depth or width.

What might be called original 9N production include the following for these model years.

1939
• A starter button on the left side of the instrument   panel near the ammeter gauge.

This close-up illustrates a smooth cast rear axle that was original at the beginning of 1939 9N production. Casting such a large piece often allowed air pockets to form in the metal, which in turn weakened the casting and resulted in later breakage under a heavy load. In mid-1940, this smooth casting was replaced by smaller diameter hubs that were hot-riveted to the axle.

• Grease fittings on the front axle extensions are on the front side.
• Two crease bars on the fender instead of one.
• Smooth, cast one-piece rear axle and hub.
• Radius rods are I-beam type on early models.
• Switch key on the right of the instrument panel near the oil pressure gauge.
• Ignition light on the left side dash below ammeter gauge.
• Both brake pedals are the same and can be interchanged.

A 1939 9N features the three-point hitch mounted plow. It's doubtful the restorer will do any plowing with this collector's piece, although the combination represents a worthwhile addition to any N-Series collection.

1940
- Hoods and metal work are now all steel.
- Introduction of hinged battery and fuel cover.
- Change to a three-brush generator, one physically larger in size although the pulley remains the same diameter.
- Early production switch key moved to the lower left side.
- Starter button moved to transmission cover.
- Safety, neutral lock out, starter adopted, starter on transmission cover, key on dash lower right side.
- Switch later moved to the lower left side of dash.
- Switch again moved to the left side of steering column.
- Freeze plug added to engine, left side center block.

1941
- Red ignition light dropped.
- Three-spoke steering wheel replaces four-spoke steering wheel.
- Steel grill with vertical bars instead of horizontal—solid center.
- Grease fittings on front axle extension changed to rear side.

- Left and right brake pedals are different, not interchangeable.

Aftermarket goodies for the 9N

Aftermarket manufactures were quick to introduce a number of items that now appear on many 9N models. These include the practical bolt-on running boards or step plates, air filter improvements, bumpers, drawbar holders, and lighting packages.

The 9N was popular with farmers, and they proved this by laying out the hard cash necessary to own one even though depression economics lingered in many areas. By the end of the first year, sales totaled in excess of 10,000 at the introductory price tag of $585. This price included generator, battery, PTO, starter, and rubber tires. Headlights were the sole factory option to be offered.

The 9N's electrical system, which did away with the temperamental magneto on most early tractors, was a godsend to farmers firing up on cold winter mornings. Not only did the starter make hand-cranking obsolete, but there was no longer any worry about the dreaded tractor engine "kick back" that caused more than one farmer to suffer a broken arm.

Notice the chromed grill with solid center bar on this early 1939 9N. Outfitted with a mounted plow, it's a definite show tractor.

Three 9Ns from consecutive model years (from left, 1941, 1940, and 1939) line-up for inspection.

The three-point hitch also avoided the formerly hazardous propensity for rearing up and flipping over. This three-point hitch was a giant step not only in the Ford-Ferguson, but also in making later generations of all succeeding tractors user friendly.

Model 9N

Year	Serial Numbers	Annual Production
1939	1 to 10233	10,233
1940	10234 to 45975	5,742
1941	45976 to 88887	2,912
1942	88888 to 99002	10,115

Model 9N Specifications

General:
- Wheelbase   70 inches at 48-inch tread width
- Front to drawbar length   115 inches
- Height   54.5 inches
- Width, normal tread   64.75 inches
- Weight, inc. gas, oil, and water; operator not included   2,410 pounds
- Front tread   48 to 76 inches in 4-inch steps
- Rear tread   48 to 76 inches in 4-inch steps
- Front tire size   4-19 4-ply
- Rear tire size, early   8-32 4-ply
- Rear tire size, late   10-28 4-ply

Capacities:
- Fuel tank   9 gallons standard
  1 gallon reserve
  10 gallons total

- Engine crankcase without filter   5 quarts
- Transmission, hydraulic, and differential 5 gallons
- Cooling system   12 quarts

Engine:
- Type   4-cylinder "L" head
- Compression ratio   6 to 1
- Displacement   119.7 cubic inches
- Maximum drawbar rating   16.3 horsepower

Transmission:
- Type   Constant mesh
- Forward speeds   3
- Reverse   1

Ignition system:
- Type   Battery
- Firing order   1-2-4-3
- Volts   6
- Ground terminal   Positive

Model 9N Color Scheme

Both the 9N and 2N took a page from Henry's Model T; buyers could have any color they wanted as long as—in this case—it was gray.

Voluminous research has turned up the following information concerning paint color schemes. There may be disagreements, however, because only a few of the expert sources around the country agree when it comes to original paint details. This list represents the best of present thinking.

"Ol' No. 16." The 1939 9N wearing serial number 16 greets the setting sun by reflecting the rich, vibrant colors from its polished aluminum hood. This tractor, quite possibly produced on the first day of 9N production, is symbolic of the impending dawn of a bright future of the N-Series tractor.

A 1939 9N sports serial number 357, which means it was one of the first N-Series tractors to leave the Ford factory—almost certainly within the first week of manufacture. It reads like a textbook on early 9Ns when you notice the horizontal bars on the grill, four-spoke steering wheel, small generator, smooth cast rear axle, and snap-in battery cover.

Engine
- Fan—gray
- Fan shroud—gray
- Radiator, tank, and cores—black
- Radiator hose—black
- Spark plugs wire, originally cloth of brown/rust color —black
- Spark plug wire tube—cadmium-plated, unpainted
- Fan belt—black
- Generator and pulley—gray
- Crankcase breather cap—gray
- Head, block, and oil pan—gray
- Starter—gray
- Wire harness, originally cloth of brown/rust color—black
- Magneto or distributor—gray
- Spark plugs—unpainted
- Battery cover—gray or polished aluminum

- Battery rack—gray
- Ground strap—unpainted
- Battery cable—black
- Fuel line, settlement bulb, and fuel shut off valve—unpainted
- Air cleaner—gray
- Oil filter—gray
- Fuel tank—cadmium-plated, unpainted
- Carburetor—gray
- Manifold—gray

Transmission
- Housing—gray
- Gearshift—gray (top four-inch chromed until 1941)
- Gearshift boot—black
- Gearshift knob—chromed
- Starter button—unpainted, chrome
- Power take off lever—gray

Right
This feature is found only on early Model 9Ns. The throttle lever is chromed all the way from the tip until it disappears into the tractor's steering column.

- Hood—gray
- Side panels—gray
- Battery cover—gray
- Toolbox—gray
- Fenders—gray
- Fender mounting bolts—gray
- Ford hood emblem—early, chrome with blue background
- Ferguson System emblem—early, chrome with blue background

A fate that befalls all too many of the original aluminum castings: the side panels have developed stress cracks. With professional help, however, the panels can be restored. Making the effort is usually well worth the time, effort, and money expended.

- Sherman transmission lever—gray
- Brake pedals—gray
- Clutch pedal—gray
- Step plates, not available from factory

Differential
- Housing—gray
- Rear axle housing—gray
- Axle hubs rear—gray
- Lug bolts and nuts—gray
- Brake drums—gray
- Three-point hitch—gray
- Hydraulic touch control lever—gray with chrome knob
- Drawbar—gray
- PTO shaft cover—gray

Front axle assembly
- Axle hubs front—gray
- Axle extension—gray
- Lug bolts and nuts—gray
- Drag link—gray
- Radius rods—gray
- Tie rods—gray

Wheels and rims
- Rear rims—zinc
- Front rims—gray

Sheet metal
- Grill—gray (early models used chromed aluminum cast)

The chrome knob on the hydraulic lift control lever and the cast-aluminum early 9N lift control quadrant.

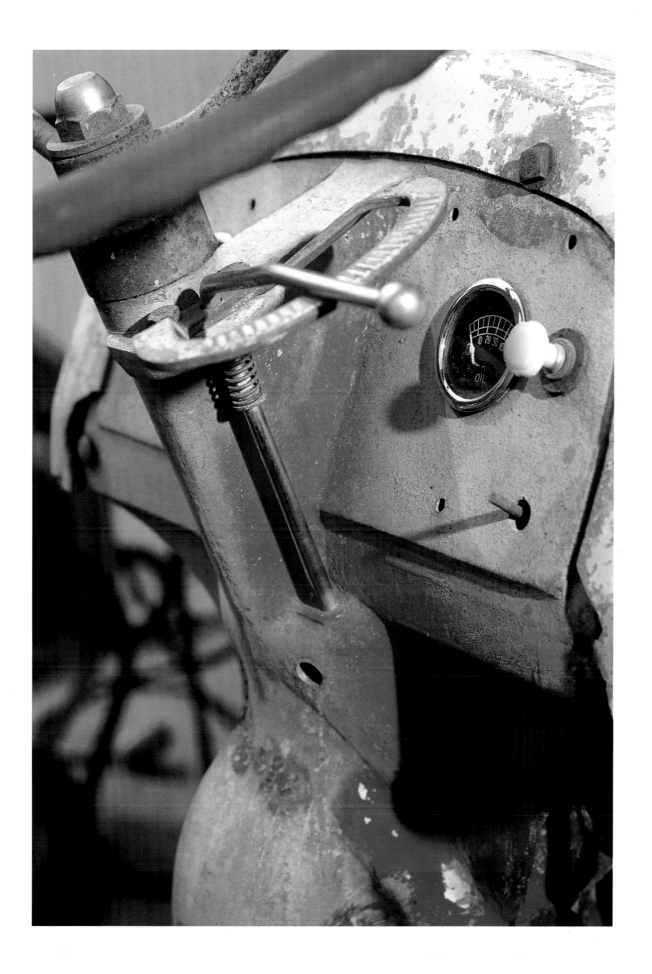

Left
An original battery cover for the 9N aluminum hood. Note that the clips holding the cover in place are one piece, side-to-side. When the original clips broke, as they were prone to do, many were replaced with a variety of homemade devices and extra holes were drilled for rivets or bolts.

- Seat and assembly—gray
- Headlights bracket—gray
- Taillight bracket—gray
- Radiator cap—chrome
- Battery cover knob—chrome or gray

Dash and instrumentation
- Dash—gray
- Switch and key—unpainted
- Choke knob—chrome or unpainted
- Throttle lever—gray with tip knob chrome
- Throttle lever base—gray
- Steering wheel center—chrome or plated acorn nut, unpainted
- Ammeter gauge bezel—chrome
- Oil pressure gauge bezel—chrome
- Ignition light bezel—chrome

Model Identification Tips

Model 9N

Serial numbers	1 to 99002
Color	All gray
Transmission	three-speed
Brake pedals	Left and right side
Factory step plates	None
Grill	Horizontal bars (early); vertical bars (late)
Hood	Cast-aluminum on steel w/clip in fuel fill cover*
Fenders	Five-bolt
Distributor	Front mount
Rear hubs	Cast, smooth*

Note: This list alone cannot unerringly identify your tractor, but it can give you a good idea at a cursory glance or walk around.

* Changes were made during production— the model could have either one depending on early or late production.

Left
This original cast-aluminum grill could have been the find of an N-Series tractor restorer's lifetime if only it had been complete.

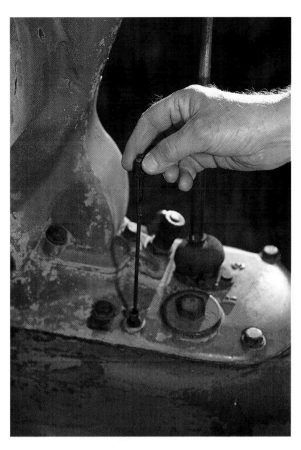

In 1940 the transmission oil check was changed from a plug on the right side of the transmission housing to the top dipstick shown.

This 1941 Ford panel truck came from the factory with the same L-head four-cylinder engine as in the 9N Ford tractor. Originally these trucks were manufactured with a 60-horsepower V-8. But possibly because of economy concerns, Ford switched some production to the smaller four-cylinder engine. This smaller engine didn't prove to be too satisfactory and most trucks so equipped saw service as city delivery vehicles where power and speed were not big factors.

Three

Model 2N

The material restrictions brought about by the gigantic World War II effort appear to be the most frequent explanation for the birth of the 2N in 1942. These "war models" draw a lot of interest. But in reality they were manufactured in extremely small numbers.

The two obvious changes are the reversions to steel wheels and magneto ignition. But these changes were neither instantaneous nor permanent because some production 2Ns exited the assembly line with rubber tires and starters.

There are two probable explanations for how this happened. One is that as government allotments became available, the line switched to the standard rubber and electrical system. The other could be due to the fact that Harry Ferguson's visit to President Franklin Roosevelt resulted in an increased materials allotment to Ford for manufacturing the Ford-Ferguson. Tractors at the time were considered essential to provide food for the war effort.

One of the subtle changes that identify the 2N model concerns the emblem. On most emblems it's almost impossible to see, especially if the emblem has received several coats of paint in the interim. If you look closely at the Ford emblem, however, "2N" is struck in the metal beneath the Ford script. The number "2" and the letter "N" are approximately the size of 12-point type, or 1/8-inch high.

This emblem on a 1945 2N shows the "2N" stamped in the metal below the Ford script. The 2N emblem is the only one of the three emblems that appear on the N-Series tractors with this identification mark. The Ferguson System badge originally didn't have blue paint on the lettering.

Left
Although far from any sugar cane or cotton fields, this rare sugar cane and cotton special is a prize for any collector.

The taillight on a 2N with an aftermarket lighting package. The lens is glass, as were all such lenses in the years before plastic became a cheaper material for production usage.

Unusual is the word for this safety device. It was installed to automatically depress the clutch pedal when the attached implement encountered an obstruction. Its manufacturer is unknown, although it does look factory made. Of course, there's a possibility this device is the work of some cautious and safety-concerned farmer. Also note the large U-bolt over the transmission housing, origin and purpose also unknown.

Production of the 2N began with rubber tires. The rear tire size was standardized to 10.00x28. For quick identification purposes, the last outwardly visible difference between the 9N and 2N concerns the radius rods. These were changed in 1944 from the I-beam design to oval tubular construction.

Original 2N production includes the following for these model years.

1942

- Designation changed to 2N.
- Equipped with pressurized radiator.

- Aluminum-plated cast radiator cap changed to painted black cast.
- Steering wheel changed to three-spoke with steel rods.
- "War model" with steel wheels, hand crank, and magneto.
- Front choke for cranking on war models.

One thing that's never been commented on, and which would be worthy of a video, is what happened on the Ford factory floor during these changes to the 2N during the war years. Anyone even vaguely familiar with mass production can only imagine the headaches that

A 1945 2N nicely set up with its original grill. By this time in production, the Ford design team had redesigned the center rib.

This 1945 2N war production model came originally equipped with factory rubber tires, generator, lighting package, and distributor. When you think of the 2N, the war model naturally comes to mind. But not all 2N tractors were built during the World War II years and delivered with steel wheels and magneto.

This Model 2N was built during World War II. Look closely on the right side panel for the hole for the choke. The operator started the tractor by cranking—because it lacked the electrical system for a starter—so the choke location at the front was a convenience, if not a complete necessity on colder days.

beset the employees—from line workers to purchasing agents—when they were required to switch from steel to rubber and back again as materials became available. Although Henry Ford was dead set against his employees drinking alcohol, no doubt more than one employee considered a hip flask as necessary "tooling" for the job. And probably more curses than prayers were heard on the factory floor each time orders were given to switch the line from one version to another.

It does speak eloquently of both the management and workers that tractors rolled off the line as regularly as they did. From 1942 to 1947, a total of 197,129 2Ns were manufactured. More than 99,000 were manufactured during the trying war years.

A rare sugarcane and cotton special converted by a kit made by the Philips foundry, Bakersfield, California. The unit is part of the Palmer Fossum, Northfield, Minnesota, collection of Ford N-Series tractors. Although not all are in restored condition, Fossum owns at least one model of each N-Series tractor produced between the inception of the 9N in 1939 through the close of production in 1952.

Model 2N

Year	Serial Numbers	Annual Production
1942	99003 to 1053742	6,372
1943	105375 to 126537	21,163
1944	126538 to 169981	43,444
1945	169982 to 198730	28,749
1946	198731 to 258503	59,773
1947	258504 to 296131	7,628

Model 2N Specifications

General:
- Wheelbase   70 inches at 48-inch tread width
- Front to drawbar length   115 inches
- Height   54.5 inches
- Width, normal tread   64.75 inches
- Weight, inc. gas, oil, and water; operator not included
                                                  2,410 pounds

This restored Moto-Tug is a B-NO-40 heavy-duty model with dual rear wheels. Made during 2N years, it was used by the military and saw action as a reliable tow tractor on either a World War II airfield or an aircraft carrier.

This 1942 2N is definitely a war model. The certain tip-offs are the handcrank and steel wheels. Visible on the right side panel is the choke rod. The solid center grill has been replaced by the later style with the four vertical cutouts.

- Front tread   48 to 76 inches in 4-inch steps
- Rear tread   48 to 76 inches in 4-inch steps
- Front tire size   4-19 4-ply
- Rear tire size   10-28 4-ply

Capacities:
- Fuel tank   9 gallons standard
                                       1 gallon reserve
                                      10 gallons total
- Engine crankcase without filter   5 quarts
- Transmission, hydraulic, and differential 5 gallons
- Cooling system   12 quarts

Engine:
- Type   4-cylinder "L" head
- Compression ratio   6 to 1
- Displacement   119.7 cubic inches
- Maximum drawbar rating   16.3 horsepower

Transmission:
- Type   Constant mesh
- Forward speeds   3
- Reverse   1

Ignition system:
- Type   Battery
- Firing order   1-2-4-3
- Volts   6
- Ground terminal   Positive

Model 2N color scheme

Research has turned up the following information concerning paint color schemes. There may be disagreements, however, because only a few of the expert sources around the country agree when it comes to original paint details. This list represents the best of present thinking.

Engine
- Fan—gray
- Fan shroud—gray
- Radiator, tank, and cores—black
- Radiator hose—unpainted black
- Spark plugs—unpainted
- Fan belt—unpainted black
- Generator and pulley—gray
- Crankcase breather cap—gray
- Head, block, and oil pan—gray
- Starter—gray
- Wire harness—unpainted
- Magneto or distributor—unpainted
- Spark plug wires, originally cloth of brown color—unpainted
- Spark plug wire tube—cadmium-plated, unpainted
- Battery cover—gray

- Battery rack—gray
- Ground strap—unpainted
- Battery cable—black
- Fuel line, settlement bulb, and fuel shut off valve—unpainted
- Air cleaner—gray
- Oil filter—gray
- Fuel tank—cadmium-plated, unpainted
- Carburetor—gray
- Manifold—gray

Transmission
- Housing—gray
- Gearshift—gray
- Gearshift boot—black
- Gearshift knob—gray
- Starter button—unpainted
- Power take off lever—gray
- Brake pedals—gray
- Clutch pedal—gray
- Running boards, not available from factory

Differential
- Housing—gray
- Rear axle housing—gray
- Axle hub—gray
- Lug bolts and nuts—gray or unpainted plating
- Brake drums—gray
- Three-point hitch—gray
- Hydraulic touch control lever—gray
- Drawbar—gray
- PTO shaft cover—gray

Front axle assembly
- Axle hub—gray
- Axle extension—gray
- Lug bolts and nuts—gray or unpainted plating
- Drag link—gray
- Radius rods—gray
- Tie rods—gray

Wheels and rims
- Rear rims—zinc plated
- Front rims—gray

Sheet metal
- Grill—gray
- Hood—gray
- Side panels—gray
- Battery cover—gray
- Toolbox—gray
- Fenders—gray
- Fender mounting bolts—gray
- Ford emblem—silver script and oval edge, blue background

A different view of the 1942 2N rolling on steel wheels.

Although not made in consecutive years, three 2Ns display much uniformity. From the left, they were manufactured in 1947, 1945, and 1942.

- Ferguson System emblem—silver letters, blue background
- Seat and assembly—gray
- Headlight mounting assembly—gray
- Taillight bracket—gray
- Radiator cap—black
- Battery cover knob—chrome or gray

Not too many B-NO-40 Moto-Tugs were produced. Notice the horn button located on the lower left of the instrument panel. Although the horn button doesn't appear to be original, it is mounted in the proper location.

Dash and instrumentation
- Dash—gray
- Switch and key—unpainted
- Choke knob—chrome or unpainted

- Throttle lever—gray
- Throttle lever base—gray
- Steering wheel center—plated acorn nut unpainted
- Ammeter gauge bezel—black
- Oil pressure gauge bezel—black

Model Identification Tips

Model 2N

Serial numbers	99003 to 296131
Color	All gray
Transmission	three-speed
Brake pedals	Left and right side
Factory step plates	None
Grill	Vertical bars
Hood	Steel with hinged fuel fill cover
Fenders	Five-bolt*
Distributor	Front mount
Rear hubs	Riveted*

Note: This list alone cannot unerringly identify your tractor, but it can give you a good idea at a cursory glance or walk around.

* Changes were made during production—the model could have either one depending on early or late production.

The horn was original equipment on this B-NO-40 Moto-Tug; although its location seems to be in conflict with the toolbox mounting location. The toolbox is missing but would have been mounted in approximately the same location as the horn is now.

This identification plate is somewhat of a mystery. Collectors and restorers believe that some of the B-NO-40 Moto-Tugs had this plate and some did not. The plate says "Harry Ferguson, Inc., Model B-NO-40, serial number 474."

A special feature of the B-NO-40 Moto-Tug was a fuel tank with a solid brass gas cap—a government specification that Ford had to comply with in order to sell these tugs to Uncle Sam.

Another government specification for the B-NO-40 Moto-Tug was this fuel strainer.

The Model 8N

A 1950 8N outfitted with a Dearborn grader that Dwight Emstrom found in New York state. He restored the grader and mounted it on this tractor, which had the honor of being the last 8N sold in his hometown of Galesburg, Illinois.

Henry Ford called it quits in 1945. He was 82 years old and in failing health. He gave up the reins of power reluctantly and probably at the insistence of his wife. His grandson, 28-year-old Henry II, stepped to the helm of the Ford ship. Saving the world's largest privately held corporation from ruin was the course he had to navigate. It was neither an easy nor enviable task for such a young man.

The decision that most affected the production of tractors occurred in late 1946 when Henry Ford II informed Harry Ferguson that the handshake agreement with his grandfather was over. Ford would supply Ferguson's distribution company with tractors only until mid-1947.

The big blow, however, was that Ford intended to establish its own marketing network—and more important, its own line of implements. Not only that, the company planned to introduce a new tractor to be known as the Ford 8N. Furthermore, this new tractor would employ the Ferguson three-point hydraulic system with little modification, absolutely no apology, and no license or royalty fees.

Ferguson's famous lawsuit was not long in being filed. But Harry didn't waste any time waiting for the courts or a settlement. With characteristic no-nonsense speed, he made arrangements for pro-

duction of his own tractor, to be known as the Ferguson TO-20.

Although this tractor looked like the 2N, it was equipped with various improvements that placed it in the category of the Ford 8N. It was a good tractor. In fact, the Ferguson TO-20 was enough of a success that this may have hurt him in his court case against Ford. Jurors possibly didn't think the Ferguson injury was all that bad.

Sales of the new 8N were brisk indeed when it was offered for sale in July 1947. More than

Left
This 1951 8N high-crop is right where it belongs, in a field of growing corn. The high-crops were not a factory issue but were converted by kits produced by aftermarket manufacturers.

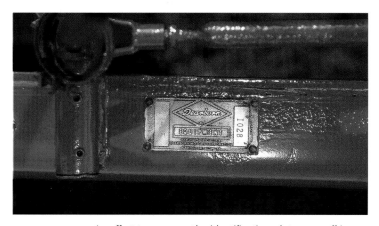

An effort to preserve the identification plate pays off in providing this grader with authenticity and a right-off-the assembly line appearance. This close-up clearly shows the Dearborn Equipment logo, serial number I028, and the manufacturer's name and address: Meili-Blumberg Corporation, New Holstein, Wisconsin, U.S.A. Note that "Pat. Pend." is also visible.

40,000 8N tractors had been manufactured and sold by the end of the year just six months later.

Two visible changes are immediately and readily recognizable on the 8N. The first is that the sheet metal is a lighter gray. Someone later observed that this lighter gray color was an effort to make bird droppings less visible. If this was indeed the reason for the color change, perhaps ultimate credit needs to be given to the lowly English sparrow. As anyone with experience housing farm equipment knows, sparrows are the curse of machine sheds, new or old. Roosting in the rafters—sometimes in the hundreds—sparrows can produce a literal hailstorm of droppings that anoint the machinery parked directly below.

The second visual 8N change added vibrant color to the engine, transmission housing, differential, and front and rear hubs. All are painted dark red, hence the 8N's nickname "red belly."

Rescued from a working retirement on a vegetable truck farm in New Jersey is a 1951 8N High Crop conversion. This particular tractor has recorded only 1,900 hours since new and mounts its original equipment 10x40 rear tires and 4x19 front tires.

This 1951 8N is all original and has been carefully and painstakingly restored to showroom condition. The result is that it looks good enough to be used for a Ford Farming advertisement. Ford-New Holland gray #MIJ-957 and Diamond Vogel red #141959 teamed up for this great paint job.

The side-mount distributor introduced in the 1950 model year. The tractor's owner points out that the fan and fan shroud are painted red, just as they appeared when they originally arrived new from the factory.

Less visible, yet a symbol of what was transpiring, was that after a decade of successful partnership, the Ferguson System emblem was gone from the front of the tractor. The new emblem was the familiar Ford script enclosed in a oval. Now, though, the blue background of the 9N and 2N Ford emblems was replaced with a red background. The new emblem was slightly larger in size too.

Mechanically there were some significant and needed changes. One was a modification that David Brown, Harry Ferguson's partner, thought was important and wanted to make on the Ferguson-Brown tractor more than a decade earlier: a four-speed transmission. Harry Ferguson argued with Brown about transmissions all during their relationship. Brown lost initially. Later, after Ferguson dissolved their partnership, Brown quickly went to a four-speed in his own new tractor. And Ferguson obviously came to recognize the need for a four-speed transmission because this was one of the features of his Ferguson TO-20 when it debuted.

The 8N also was introduced to the world with a four-speed transmission. Coupled with a bit more powerful engine—compression ratio increased slightly from 6:1 up to 6.37:1—the performance of the 8N was vastly improved both in the field and on the road.

Perhaps the most appreciated change for the tractor operator was that finally both brake pedals were on the right side of the tractor. Running boards were also provided as standard equipment, a feature probably even more appreciated by most operators than relocation of the brake pedals.

Two changes appeared on the three-point hydraulic system. First, a position control was added to the automatic depth control, which was standard on the original Ferguson System. This control lever was located under the seat next to the hydraulic control lever. When engaged, this positive control overrode the automatic depth control, keeping the implement at a constant depth.

During the 8N's life, the hydraulic lift rocker had either one, two, or three position holes. The draft control system was originally designed for plowing. However, as the many new implements were added to the line, different degrees of leverage against the control system were experienced. By adding more holes

Follow the gas line up to the bottom of the fuel tank and, just above the spark plug, you can see the anti-rattle grommet. The tractor's owner confirmed that this was an original 1951 8N factory issue.

on the lift rocker, the operator could adjust for different soil density and other variables. The heavier the pull on the implement, the lower the position used, as a rule. Theoretically, the lighter the drag on the implement the higher the top link should be attached.

The steering was also changed from a sector gear design to a recalculating ball mechanism. Combined with the steering improvement was a change in height and pitch of the steering wheel.

The Ford script was embossed on each side of the hood toward the front. This script was painted red to contrast better with the light gray metal. Sometime later in 1949, the same script was added to the fenders.

A notable addition, the "Proofmeter," was added to the instrument panel in early 1950. It was the forerunner of today's even more complex yet standard gauges that pinpoint engine performance.

The last 8N rolled off the Highland Park plant in December 1952. It carried serial number 524076, give or take a few numbers.

In 1939 the 9N was introduced, carrying a price tag of $585. The price of the last 8N was approximately $1,200, and not all that much more expensive considering the effects of wartime inflation. All told, the N-Series tractor had remained affordable enough that a total of 884,469 of the three models were purchased and put to work around the world. The N Series had experienced a good run.

Model 8N

Year	Serial Numbers	Annual Production
1947	1 to 37907	37,908
1948	37908 to 141369	103,462
1949	141370 to 245636	104,267
1950	245637 to 363592	117,956
1951	363593 to 442034	78,442
1952	442035 to 524076	82,042

Model 8N Specifications

General:
- Wheelbase   70 inches at 48-inch tread width
- Front to drawbar length   115 inches
- Height   54.5 inches
- Width, normal tread   64.75 inches
- Weight, inc. gas, oil and water; operator not included 2,410 pounds.

Nicely done rear wheel and tire on an 8N. Notice that the rim has been painted aluminum (originally it was zinc-plated), and the wheel disc has been painted gray like the rest of the sheet metal. The axle hub and lug bolts are red. However, the lug nuts themselves remain unpainted. Why? That's the way the owner says it was done originally. The lug nuts are plated.

Dash shot of a 1951 8N shows the black plastic gearshift knob and the three-spoke steering wheel held with the plated acorn nut. By the way, the plastic gearshift knob is rumored to have been manufactured from a plastic derived from soybeans. Anyhow, it's a fact that Henry Ford did extensive soybean research on his experimental farm near Dearborn, Michigan.

- Front tread   48 to 76 inches in 4-inch steps
- Rear tread   48 to 76 inches in 4-inch steps
- Front tire size   4-19 4-ply
- Rear tire size   10-28 4-ply

Capacities:
- Fuel tank   9 gallons. standard
  1 gallons. reserve
  10 gallons. total
- Engine crankcase without filter   5 quarts
- Transmission, hydraulic and differential 5 gallons
- Cooling system   12 quarts

Engine:
- Type   4-cylinder "L" head
- Compression ratio, early   6 to 1
- Compression ratio, late   6.37 to 1
- Displacement   119.7 cubic inches
- Maximum drawbar rating   23.2 horsepower

Transmission:
- Type   Constant mesh
- Forward speeds   4
- Reverse   1

Ignition system:
- Type   Battery
- Firing order   1-2-4-3
- Volts   6
- Ground   Positive

Model 8N Color Scheme

You have to wonder if Henry Ford approved of the bold move to add bright red to the color scheme of the 8N. Was this the first color paint other than black and gray to get outside the door of the Ford tractor plant?

Harold L. Brock in the *9N-2N-8N Newsletter* (volume 3, number 4) provides insight to this color choice:

Snowplows were a fairly common addition in cooler climates, although this big V-plow is a bit ambitious for a stock Model 8N.

In designing the 8N we believed it important to present the product in what we hoped would be a more attractive color and identify it as different from the previous models.

In selecting the color it was my proposal to management that the chassis be painted a shade of red, as quite often the iron castings of axle, transmission, and engine block would bleed through the gray and show a rust color.

A lighter shade was felt desirable for the hood and fenders to reduce the tendency of dust and other materials (chickens like to roost on tractors) to create a discolored appearance. The proposal met with approval and the colors have proved to be durable and attractive.

The red and gray colors certainly set the 8N apart from the tractors produced under the handshake agreement and, perhaps more importantly, from Harry Ferguson's TO 20 that soon appeared on the scene.

The "red belly" 8N has some special painting considerations.

Engine
• Fan—red
• Fan shroud—red
• Radiator—all black
• Radiator hose—black
• Spark plugs—unpainted
• Fan belt—black
• Generator and pulley—red
• Crankcase breather cap—red
• Head, block, and oil pan—red
• Starter—red
• Wire harness—unpainted
• Distributor—red with black cap
• Spark plug wires—unpainted
• Spark plug wire tube—cadmium-plated
• Battery cover—gray
• Battery rack—red
• Ground strap—unpainted

A 1952 8N high-crop made from a kit by a different manufacturer than the 1951 high-crop shown in another photograph. Compare the rear wheels on the two, and it appears highly likely it was produced by the same manufacturer that made the conversion kit for the sugarcane special also shown in another photograph.

- Battery cable—unpainted
- Fuel line, settlement bulb, and fuel shut-off valve—unpainted
- Air cleaner—red
- Oil filter—red
- Fuel tank—cadmium-plated, unpainted
- Carburetor—red
- Manifold—red

Transmission
- Housing—red
- Gearshift—early, red with cast knob painted red
- Gearshift boot—black
- Gearshift knob—later, black plastic

- Starter button—plated, unpainted
- Power take off lever—red
- Brake pedals—red
- Clutch pedal—red
- Running boards—red

Differential
- Housing—red
- Rear axle housing—red
- Axle hub—red
- Lug bolts and nuts*
- Brake drums—red
- Three-point hitch—red
- Hydraulic touch control lever—red

- Drawbar—red
- PTO shaft cover—red

Front axle assembly
- Axle hub—red
- Spindle housing—red
- Lug bolts and nuts*
- Drag link—red
- Radius rods—red
- Tie rods—red

Wheels and rims
- Rear rims—zinc-plated and unpainted or dull aluminum
- Front rims—gray

Sheet metal
- Grill—gray
- Hood—gray
- Side panels—gray
- Battery cover—gray
- Toolbox—red
- Fenders—gray
- Fender mounting bolts—unpainted
- Ford emblem—silver script and raised edge on oval, red background
- Ferguson System badge—gone from 8N
- Seat and assembly—black
- Headlights brackets—gray
- Taillight brackets—gray
- Radiator cap—black
- Battery cover knob—black

Dash and instrumentation
- Dash—red
- Switch and key—unpainted
- Choke knob—unfinished or black
- Throttle lever—cadmium-plated
- Throttle lever base—cadmium-plated
- Steering wheel nut or cover—plated acorn nut, unpainted
- Ammeter gauge bezel—black
- Oil pressure gauge bezel—black
- Ignition light—none
- Proof meter bezel—black
* See text for additional information.

Model Identification Tips

Model 8N
Serial numbers	1 to 524076
Color	Light gray sheet metal with "red belly"
Transmission	four-speed
Brake pedals	Both on right side
Factory step plates	Yes

A 1952 8N with colorful, mounted cordwood saw seems too pretty to take to the woods and put to work. But the results of sawing firewood will be appreciated and enjoyed by friends and family come winter cold and accompanying snows.

David Hills, Salina, Kansas, can be proud of his restored 8N. His story is like the ones you read and hear about but that never seem to happen to you. David and his father purchased some farm property. Guess what was hidden in a dark corner of the barn on the place? Yes, this tractor!

Grill	Vertical bars
Hood	Steel with hinged fuel fill cover
Fenders	Three-bolt
Distributor	Side mount
Rear hubs	Bolted

Note: This list alone cannot unerringly identify your tractor, but it can give you a good idea at a cursory glance or walk around.

A family heirloom, this 1950 8N sits proudly on the Kansas prairie, and possibly reflect on days passed when it mowed hay in this same field as a working tractor. It was restored for Chester Todd by Johnny Grist of Topeka, Kansas.

Chester Todd's 1950 8N, serial number 278732. This tractor and an early 1947 8N helped rear Todd and his four brothers on a row crop farm near Maple Hill, Kansas—it's been in his family since the original purchase. Todd acquired it from the estate and had it restored in 1994. His father bought his first N-Series tractor in 1947; he bought the one pictured here in 1950 and yet a third 8N in 1951. Yes, it was a Ford family.

While it can't mow the grass or gather the attention of tractor show enthusiasts, models such as this one are certainly less expensive to obtain, not to mention being maintenance-free. This metal model is owned by one of the authors. It replaces a plastic model that predated it by several decades.

Left
This 8N is equipped with the three-hole upper draft control mounting mechanism. The three-hole version is said to have been introduced late in 8N production. 8Ns could be equipped with either one-, two-, or three-hole versions.

Model Identification

If you want to buy a Ford N-Series tractor, or if you already own one, your first item of business is to determine which N model you're looking at. There are some quick ways to begin, although in the long run you should check several identification points and not rely on just one.

Over the years, in many tractors the engines were replaced and old parts were upgraded with new designs. Also today, many of the N-Series tractors are being parted together from tractors relegated to the scrap heap.

Beware: There's more than one Ford tractor out there that contains parts of all three models, a "hybrid" 928N if you will.

This doesn't mean such mongrels are bad tractors. They'll still work fine for cutting the grass or plowing small fields. But you should know what you're buying or already own if your primary interest is like-new restoration of the tractor.

Caution: Even if you see a paint job that's "all gray" or that features a "red belly" don't bet the farm on a positive identification. However, up close you can usually determine if the tractor is original or simply somebody's idea of repainting at some point during the 50-plus years since the tractor rolled out of the factory.

A fine example of the multi-varied combination of replacement parts that can eventually gravitate to just one tractor. First, notice that while the tractor has an aluminum hood, the engine serial number indicates the engine has been changed. The tractor has also been painted in 8N colors. The tire rims are early one-piece, the axle hubs are hot-riveted, and the wheel disc is hat rim. Still, even with all these additions, it's a desirable restoration tractor.

Left
You may not know for sure what you're looking at when you first spot this nicely restored N tractor--but you know you'd like to have one like it. This is Dwight Emstrom's 1945 2N outfitted with a set of sand wheels and some other goodies.

Restorer Dwight Emstrom, Galesburg, Illinois, rolls out some of his favorite N-Series Ford tractors to greet a beautiful summer day. The foreground tractor is the 1939 9N Serial Number 16 with aluminum hood; its followed by a 1952 8N with cordwood saw on the three-point hitch, an original condition 1945 2N, a 1945 2N with sand wheels, a 1939 9N serial number 175 with polished aluminum hood, a 1948 8N high-crop, a 1939 9N with three-point mounted plow, a 1942 Moto-Tug, and a 1951 8N high-crop.

A set of sand wheels is mounted on this 1945 2N. The rear tires are original Firestone 10x20s. These sand wheels can be locked out, as they are in this photograph, when there's no need for the added traction. As their name implies, in extremely sandy conditions that require extra traction, when unlocked these sand wheels swing down with the rotation of the wheel. Traction becomes similar to using a set of steel lugs.

Also, many Ford N-Series tractors have been painted yellow or orange, perhaps when the machines were used for road maintenance . Be forewarned that folks out there are painting N-Series tractors in all sorts of unusual combinations. You might spot an 8N with its original colors reversed. It'll have a red hood and sheet metal with a gray belly. There's even a working 8N with a formerly red belly that a proud Irish descendant had painted shamrock green.

Steering wheels differed over the years too. Remember, however, that steering wheels are easy to replace. Steering wheels only help determine the model and year if you're fairly sure the unit is an original tractor. The 9N started with a four-spoke steering wheel that fea-

The original intent of this photograph of an original and nicely restored 1945 2N was to show the front head lamps that were such a popular option. But, surprise, even the restoration pros sometimes make mistakes. Or perhaps the factory provided the experienced restorers with a rare production line irregular. Regardless, notice that the head lamp mounting plate is on upside down.

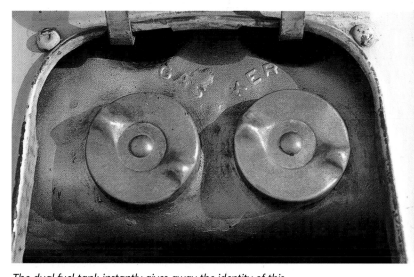

The dual fuel tank instantly gives away the identity of this unusual N-Series tractor. It's a 1952 8NAN. Another name for it is the "kero burner," meaning it has the capability to run on kerosene. Although it never was a big seller in the United States, many were sold to foreign markets, especially Great Britain, where the price of kerosene was considerably cheaper than that of gasoline.

The manifold on the 1952 8NAN kerosene burner is different from the one on a straight gasoline engine. The manifold was designed to run hotter for complete ignition of the kerosene fuel. The tractor was always started on gasoline, allowed to warm up, and then was switched to burning kerosene.

An aftermarket item, the Dowden foot accelerator on this 8N allows the operator to change tractor engine speeds with a foot, just like in an automobile or pickup. The accelerator was manufactured by the Dowden Manufacturing Company, Prairie City, Iowa.

tured a center chrome cap. This changed to a three-spoke wheel in 1940. All 2Ns came with a three-spoke steering wheel that utilized metal rods. The three spoke wheels are held in place with a single plated acorn nut. The 8N was a three-spoker, but the rods are made of the same material as the wheel's rim.

The transmissions interchange between all 9N and 2N models. A point to check is the transmission gearshift lever. The black plastic gearshift knob didn't show up until the late 8N models. The early 8Ns had a small cast knob just like the 9N and 2N. Until 1941, the early 9N gear shift levers are chrome for the top 4 inches of the lever, including the small cast knob.

That it took a period of eight years to move both brake pedals to the right side is hard to understand once you've operated a Ford tractor set up like this or with the brakes as originally furnished with one to a side.

An even bigger mystery is why Ford or Ferguson didn't adapt the step plate or running board as standard for those same eight years. Surely someone in their organizations had to know about the availability and popularity of these units on the aftermarket. Even homemade running boards were plentiful, because they made climbing on and off the tractor so much less stressful, not to mention safer. A good guess would be that 80 to 90 percent of unrestored 9N and 2N tractors have some type of aftermarket running board attached to them. Like the brake pedals, these helpful and considerate improvements weren't adopted until the 8N's introduction in 1947.

Look over a number of unrestored Ns of any vintage and you'll have no trouble spotting numerous dents and bruises on the front of the tractor, especially the grill. Hedge rows, tree limbs, other machinery in the machine shed, feed bunks, and gate posts all seem to have an attraction for the Ford grills. That's why there's a better than even chance that the grill you're looking at isn't the same grill that rolled off the assembly line with the tractor.

Hoods, too, aren't as straightforward as you would think. They all look like a typical Ford tractor hood—but only until you check them out with the real old-timers or restoration pros who have an eye for the differences. One size fits all is true with the hoods through all the years of Ford tractor manufacture. The only exception is with the aluminum hood and early steel hoods on the 9N that didn't have the later two through-mounting bolts on the bottom of the side panels.

Where the distributor is mounted on the engine can help you nail down the model and year of the tractor. Starting with the 9N, the distributor

The rear work light is mounted on the right rear fender. It swivels 360 degrees and can be moved either up and down.

is mounted at the center front of the engine block. It stayed in the same location until into the production run of the 8N. During 1950, the 8N distributor was moved from center front of the block to the right front mounting where it remained. This is sometimes referred to as the side-mount or angle-mount distributor.

Hubs and rims can certainly be confusing to someone new to Ford tractors. If it makes you feel better, sometimes even those well-versed in "Fordology" have their disagreements over this issue.

The early production model 9Ns are equipped with a smooth, cast one-piece hub and axle. Another term for this is the "pie axle." These proved prone to twisting off (hubs were hot-riveted to the axle in 1941). Later, if the hub or axle had to

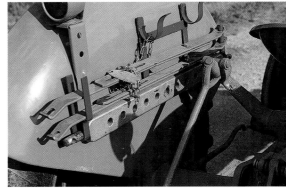

This aftermarket attachment allows the operation of the tractor from the ground rather than from the usual mid-tractor seat. The clutch and steering can be operated while the operator is off the tractor doing handling chores, such as picking up hay bales from the field. With today's litigious society, it's doubtful any company would dare market a product that might even remotely hinder safety.

The drawbar fender brackets and grease gun bracket keep these items ready for use.

The PTO-mounted grindstone is an accessory that came in handy to sharpen anything on the farm from the kitchen butcher knife to the dulled knives of a silage cutter.

be replaced, bolts were substituted for the rivets attaching the hub to the axle.

All 2Ns were originally manufactured with riveted hubs. Over the years, whenever a smooth cast hub twisted from the axle, it was usually replaced with the riveted 2N type.

The 8N axle is different yet, being threaded on the outer end. The hub was secured with a nut and snap ring.

Serial numbers on the engine block are generally a reliable method of determining the engine's year of manufacture, but with some exceptions. Because there are incidents where stolen tractors have had their serial numbers altered, it's a good idea to know the engine serial numbers that should go with the 9N, 2N, and 8N models. For example, be suspicious of any 9N with an added digit, making a total of six digits. This checking method isn't surefire, however. The number may be legitimate because some re-manufactured engines had their serial numbers re-stamped to different numbers.

On all N-Series engines, the serial numbers are on the tractor's left side approximately center of the block just below the cylinder head. (Left and right of the tractor is determined as if you're sitting in the tractor's driver's seat.) The only exception to this serial number location is on extremely early model 9Ns. Dwight Emstrom's 9N sports serial number 16. The serial number on this early tractor is further back near the rear of the block.

Model Identification Tips

	9N	2N	8N
Serial numbers	1 to 99002	99003 to 296131	1 to 524076
Color	All gray	All gray	Light gray sheet metal with "red belly"
Transmission	three-speed	three-speed	four-speed
Brake pedals	Left and right side	Left and right side	Both on right side
Factory step plates	None	None	Yes
Grill	Horizontal bars	Vertical bars	Vertical bars
Hood	Aluminum or steel with lip in fuel fill cover*	Steel with hinged fuel fill cover	Steel with hinged fuel fill cover
Fenders	Five-bolt	Five-bolt*	Three-bolt
Distributor	Front mount	Front mount	Side mount*
Rear hubs	Cast, smooth*	Riveted*	Bolted

Note: This list alone cannot unerringly identify your tractor, but it can give you a good idea at a cursory glance or walk around.

* Changes were made during production—the model could have either one depending on early or late production

The front axle extension originally had the grease fitting on the front side, as shown in this photograph. The grease fitting was later switched to the back side where it was less prone to damage from dirt.

Possibly a Howard transmission on a 2N tractor. This transmission, used with digger and trenching equipment, was geared to reduce ground speed to fit the capabilities of the equipment. Gear reduction could slow the ground speed to that of a turtle's pace at approximately 0.3 miles per hour.

The radiator cap on Model 2Ns.

A temporary reversion to the use of magnetos, as on this 2N wartime tractor, helped save materials for the enlarging war effort. Mature Ford tractor buffs will also recall meat ration points, sugar rationing, gas stickers, and an almost complete lack of rubber replacement tires.

Right
Dwight Emstrom proudly poses with his line-up of selected N-Series tractors.

The early 9N transmission oil check plug is located on the lower right side of the transmission housing. All 1939 and early 1940 9Ns utilized this method of checking the crankcase oil level. Only in the second model year, 1940, was an oil dipstick introduced to make this daily chore more efficient and accurate.

This original 9N shows the right side brake pedal. On early models through the mid-1940 model, the right and left brake pedals were interchangeable. While this almost certainly saved the Ford company a little money, placement of one brake pedal on each side of the tractor was neither logical nor well-liked by operators.

The left side brake pedal is exactly the same as the right brake pedal on the other side of the tractor.

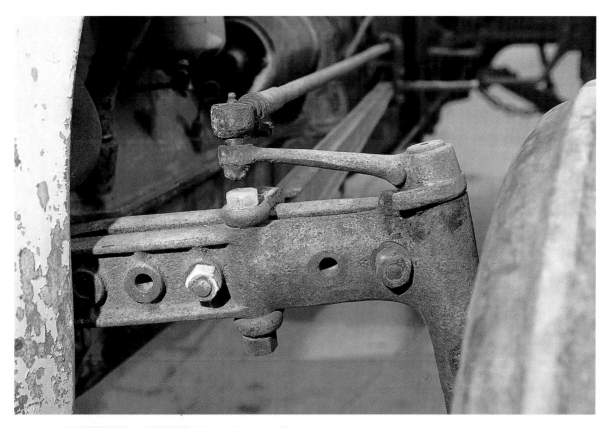

The radius rod front attachment point on this 9N is bolted to the front axle extension—which was true on all 9N and 2N models. With the introduction of the 8N, though, the radius rod was attached to the front axle itself.

This early model 9N features cast dash, steering column, and transmission cover. Not only that, but the gear-shift knob is chrome, as are the top 4 inches of the lever.

This early 9N steering column is stamped "562." Later models, however, attached the identification plate in this location.

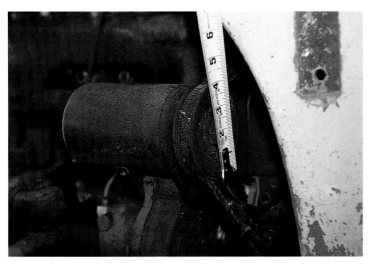

Original early 9N generator illustrates that the pulley and generator body are exactly the same diameter.

This 8N generator is the three-brush type introduced in 1940 on the 9N. While the pulley is the same size as the smaller generator pulley, the generator body is larger.

Standing at attention, these N-Series radiators are, from left: new pressurized, original 2N pressurized, original 9N non-pressurized, and one that fits a Funk conversion. The bigger capacity radiator was necessary to properly cool the heat produced by the much larger engine of the conversion.

N-Series tractor radiators line-up, from left: New pressurized for all tractors, original 2N non-pressurized model, original 9N with large top reservoir, and a Funk conversion kit radiator.

At left is an original toolbox for the 9N and 2N. At right is the 8N toolbox that was mounted under the battery cover on the engine side of the dash and column.

Early spindle arm without the key way and key; the tightening bolt is on the inside toward the tractor. This arrangement was prone to loosening with use, and so it often caused considerable undesirable steering wobble.

The redesigned and greatly improved spindle arm with a key way on the inside and with the tightening bolt moved to the outside.

Top is the old-style spindle arm without the key. Bottom is the new spindle arm with the key way and bolt on the outside.

With the introduction of the 8N, the radius rods'
attachment point was moved to the front axle itself. Up
until then, on the 9N and 2N, the radius rods were bolted
to the axle extensions.

How the Ford radiator cap evolved and matured is illustrated
from lower left to top right: Polished cast-aluminum for the
9N non-pressurized system, painted cast-aluminum cap for
the non-pressurized system, stamped steel for the pressurized
system introduced in 1942, and a new aftermarket cap for
the pressurized system.

PTO covers evolved and changed along with the N-Series
tractors. This comparison displays the different covers.
From left: a 9N cast aluminum, a 9N and 2N cast-iron,
an 8N stamped steel, and a new aluminum cover.

On the left is a side-mount magneto that would
interchange with a side-mount distributor on an 8N. On
the right is a front-mount magneto.

The Ferguson System emblem (on the bottom), the 9N and 2N Ford emblems, and the early 8N emblems were all cast. The later 8N emblem on top is stamped steel, however.

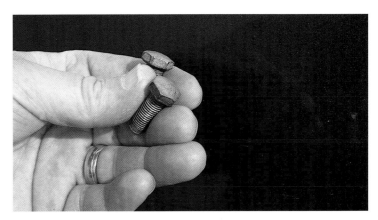

Two examples of original dome-headed bolts used to attach the instrument panel on the 8N tractors.

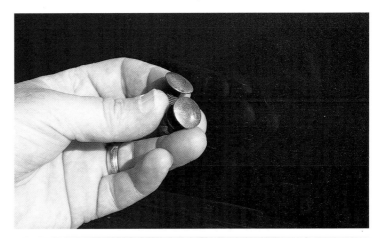

These original round-headed bolts, similar to the head on a carriage bolt, were used to attach the instrument panel on the 9N and 2N tractors.

A long lever on the right side of the transmission housing shows that this 8N has the added flexibility of the Hupp transmission. The success of the Sherman transmission no doubt prompted other manufacturers to enter the market with their own versions of the step-up or step-down transmission that many N-Series tractor owners considered essential.

Although this tire, rim, and wheel disc is a two-piece rim, the rim had no zinc plating. The wheel disc is for a smooth cast axle that was discontinued in 1940; but the two-piece rim was introduced in 1942. You can make two conclusions from these facts. First, "original" can often be difficult to establish. Second, zinc-plating of rims possibly didn't begin until sometime after 1942.

Attention is directed at the joint on a two-piece rim that was introduced in 1942. Although this rim and disc are badly weathered, they show no indication of ever being zinc-plated.

Another interesting combination on rims, hubs, and wheel discs. Note that the colors are 8N, but the hot-riveted hub says 2N with a hat rim wheel disc on a two-piece rim.

This is all 8N, with two-piece rim, standard wheel disc, and the standard threaded axle with nut.

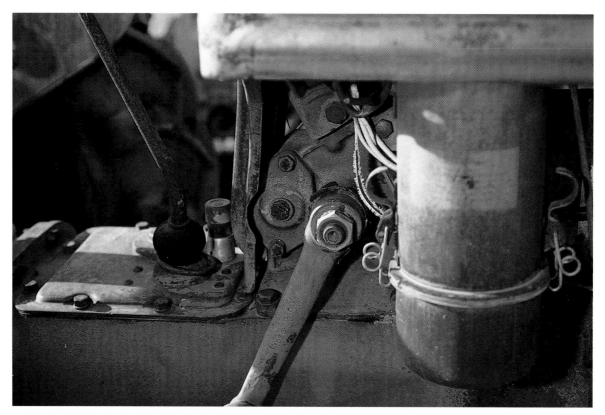

The 8N discontinued the sector gear steering setup that was used on the 9N and 2N. The new Saginaw screw and recirculating ball nut type saw two versions. Here you see the second version used after serial number 216988. The adjustment screw is visible on the steering gear housing end cover to the left of the steering geararm. This 8N carries serial number 231500. Normally, it would have a "Proofmeter," although this particular tractor does not.

N-Series radiator fans line-up, from left: Six-blade push, six-blade pull, and a four-blade pull. Fans changed during production—and even by dealerships and by owners. As a result, whatever fan is on a tractor does not guarantee it is original. The Ford-New Holland Parts Catalog issued in 1994 still lists both a six-blade pusher-type fan and a six-blade pull-type fan. The catalog notes that the latter is for torrid zones.

This shows the early 8N Saginaw screw and recirculating ball nut type steering design utilized before serial number 216988. Adjustment is made by rotating the steering gear housing cover. The engine in this tractor has been changed, so the serial numbers don't fall into the right category. The tractor doesn't have the standard "Proofmeter."

Notice the downward curve in the mounting bar on this original Ford tractor bumper. None of the several aftermarket bumpers have this downward curve.

Looked at side-by-side, the aftermarket bumper and the original are almost identical. The only exception is the downward curve in the original Ford bumper's mounting bar.

The input shaft on the right is early 9N with straight-cut gears; at left is the helical-cut gears that came later. Unless you have the correct matching gear for a Sherman transmission, it won't fit the 9N with straight-cut gears.

This wrench, which came with all N-Series tractors as part of their original equipment, had a dual purpose. In addition to being a wrench, it was also a primitive gas gauge, thanks to its markings. The smaller end can be inserted into the gas tank to check the depth of gasoline remaining in the tank—the wrench's larger end is too large to fit the gas tank so there's no way you can drop the wrench into the tank. The wrench could be used to quickly measure furrow depth or furrow width too.

The identification plate on the front upright of this cab shows the Dearborn Farm Equipment logo, Model 23-1, serial number 1699.

Six

Sherman Transmissions and Funk Conversions

You can't talk with restorers and owners or nose around an N Series "nesting ground" long before you run into two of the most common options that found their way onto these tractors.

One is the Sherman transmission. A good guess would be that four of every ten 9N and 2N tractors feature this aftermarket transmission. Why? Because necessity is the mother of invention. The three-speed transmission standard on the 9N and 2N was much too restrictive for many field work operations. And third gear certainly couldn't be viewed as any sort of road gear.

The Sherman Brothers Manufacturing Company, Royal Oaks, Michigan, first introduced its Overdrive, which was followed by the Underdrive, and later the Combination (overdrive, underdrive, and direct drive). Incidentally, the Sherman Company also supplied equipment for Ford's Fordson and for Harry Ferguson's line of equipment that fit the Ferguson System.

The other popular conversion required replacing the standard flathead four-cylinder engines with more powerful engines. The total number of conversions to six- and eight-cylinder engines is estimated to be between 5,000 to 10,000. Aircraft manufacturer

One of seven hand-built V8 conversions done in 1949-1950 by Delbert Heusinkveld. This particular tractor is No. 3. Delbert can account for four others but, two remain unaccounted for. Kind of gives one the urge to peek in every abandoned barn or shed you pass.

Take a good look at this Sherman transmission shift lever on a 1945 2N. The chrome knob on the transmission shift lever and the shape of the lever itself aren't reliable methods of identifying the transmission that's installed in the tractor. According to the Sherman Installation sheet from Sherman Products, Inc., Royal Oak, Michigan, issued April 15, 1948, this would probably be one of their Step-Up Transmissions. Models for Step-Up transmission could be either a 10A100B, which replaced A100, or 10A230B, which replaced B100.

The V-8 emblem isn't an original Ford tractor item nor was it part of the Funk conversion kit. However, the farmer making the conversion to V-8 power thought the emblem certainly belonged on the grill of his tractor sporting the conversion. He ran across the V-8 emblem at a salvage yard.

Funk Aircraft Company, Coffeyville, Kansas, produced these conversions in three models: Flathead six-cylinder, overhead valve six cylinder, and flathead V-8. It's these latter conversions to that are generating a growing swell of interest among collectors and restorers these days.

Guess what? Several years ago these conversions were considered a liability and some tractors were re-converted back to their original flathead, four-cylinder, classic N-Series engines.

Today, though, collectors are actively searching for and buying Funk conversions. Prices are trending sharply higher as a result. In addition, a new issue of conversion parts has hit the market, with approximately 100 units already sold. Conversions seem to have found real popularity at last.

Ford dealerships have provided collectors with many shop manuals, parts lists, and advertising material. However, the Sherman transmission and the Funk conversions apparently didn't provide a large volume of material with their units. So unfortunately, not many of these original parts lists, shop manuals, or sales brochures have survived.

The custom bench seat is on the third hand-built V-8 conversion fabricated by Delbert Huesinkveld, Sioux Center, Iowa. Not only is this a comfortable seat, but under the seat cushion is the tractor's gas tank. By moving the gas tank to the seat area, Huesinkveld didn't have to raise the hood to make clearance for the hefty Ford industrial V-8 engine. This preserved the tractor's original clean lines.

Above and next page
Quinton Nilson, at the time from Akron, Iowa, plows at the 1949 National Terracing Contest. The tractor? A Ford 8N. The engine? A Ford V-8 conversion. Taking home the winner's award? No contest. Nilson and his V-8 conversion easily won over a field of competitors operating big tractors.

Thankfully, some can still be found to help the collector or restorer. Several of the resources listed in the Appendix can provide some reprints of original printed material.

Sherman Transmissions

The Sherman Company had a long history with Ford and they played a quiet but significant role in the Ford-Ferguson agreement. Brothers Eber and George Sherman of New York were ambitious Fordson dealers who knew Henry Ford well.

Harry Ferguson was seeking manufacturing companies to build his plow with the Duplex Hitch designed for the Fordson tractor. Harry didn't feel the English manufacturers could produce in the quantities he anticipated needing.

The Sherman brothers and Ferguson struck a deal in 1925, establishing the Ferguson-Sherman Corporation. The company didn't enjoy a long or prosperous life. In 1927, U.S. production of the Fordson stopped, and the Ferguson-Sherman Corporation folded.

Undaunted, Ferguson pressed on with improved designs for his plow and plans to build his own tractor. The Sherman brothers imported the English Fordson and remained in business.

In early 1938, Ferguson had developed a tractor in a partnership with David Brown. When Ferguson was ready to demonstrate the tractor and the three-point attachment system, he shrewdly made sure that one of the Sherman brothers was present to observe. As Ferguson hoped, the Sherman brother reported to Henry

Delbert Huesinkveld's V-8 engine conversion is at the Funk Aircraft Company's facility in Coffeyville, Kansas. In 1949 Huesinkveld hauled the unit to Kansas hoping to interest the Funk brothers in offering a V-8 kit to go with the six-cylinder kit they already had on the market. The Funks decided to add a V-8 kit to their line of conversion kits, although production was in limited numbers.

Quinton Nilson is offered both awards and congratulations as the winner of the 1949 National Terrace contest. Nilson won the contest by plowing with his much more powerful than original Ford 8N V-8 conversion.

Ford that the tractor and hitch system were worth further examination.

The result, of course, was the Model 9N. Once the 9N was launched, it became evident that a more versatile transmission would be a big improvement. The Sherman brothers soon built the Sherman auxiliary transmission. The unit was a runaway success, and more than 100,000 Sherman transmissions were sold by the late 1940s.

The transmission was designed to fit into the housing between the engine and the factory transmission. Installation was relatively simple, and the only exterior evidence was a shift lever.

Delbert Huesinkveld with the third hand-built V-8 conversion that his brother, cousins, and he built in 1949–1950 when living at Springfield, South Dakota. The tractor served many years working on someone else's farm before Huesinkveld was able to own it for a second time. This tractor's paint is the popular Ford-New Holland gray #MIJ-957 and the red is Diamond Vogel #141959.

Huesinkveld used the Ford industrial engine as this plate on his conversion indicates. His V-8 conversion more than doubled the horsepower of the original equipment Ford four-cylinder engine.

The Sherman unit made the standard Ford transmission a multi-range unit. The step-down model gave the operator the choice of using the standard gear, or flipping the lever of the Sherman transmission to activate a low range useful for heavy pulling or fieldwork. A step-up unit effectively created a high range useful for road travel, while a more deluxe step-down and

Sherman Transmission Chart

Step-Down Ratio	1.513 to 1
Standard Ratio	1 to 1
Step-Up Ratio	0.669 to 1
Weight	54 pounds
Oil Capacity	2 pints
Shimming Provisions	mounting-flange shims

Sherman Transmission Gear Ratios for Model 9N and 2N

Gear	1,000 rpm		1,500 rpm		1,750 rpm		Full throttle	
	GS	PTO	GS	PTO	GS	PTO	GS	PTO
Standard 1st	1.79	363	2.69	545*	3.14	636	4.07	825
Step-Up 1st	3.44	543*	5.17	815	6.04	951	7.82	1,233
Step-Down 1st	1.18	240	1.78	360	2.07	420	2.69	545*
Standard 2nd	2.68	543*	4.02	815	4.69	951	6.08	1,233
Step-Up 2nd	5.34	363	8.01	545*	9.34	636	12.12	825
Step-Down 2nd	1.53	240	2.29	360	2.67	420	3.46	545*
Standard 3rd	3.53	240	5.29	360	6.17	420	8.01	545*
Step-Up 3rd	7.98	543*	11.97	815	13.96	951	18.12	1,233
Step-Down 3rd	2.31	363	3.46	545*	4.04	636	5.23	825
	2.87							
Standard Reverse	1.92	363	2.88	545*	3.36	636	4.36	825
Step-Up Reverse	2.87	543*	4.31	815	5.02	951	6.52	1,233
Step-Down Reverse	1.27	240	1.90	260	2.22	420	2.88	545*

GS=ground speed in miles per hour   PTO=power take-off rpm

* ASAE standard PTO speed for PTO tools.
**Full-throttle speeds shown are at an engine speed of 2269 RPM, which is well sithin the adjustable range of the governor. Engine speed as low as 2,190 puts the "Step-Down" PTO speed within the ASAE standard range of 526 to 546 RPM.

Sherman Transmission Gear Ratios for Model 8N

Gear	1,000 rpm		1,500 rpm		1,750 rpm		Full throttle	
	GS	PTO	GS	PTO	GS	PTO	GS	PTO
Step-Down 1st	1.32	240	1.83	340	2.13	420	2.77	545*
Step-Down 2nd	1.57	240	2.35	360	2.74	420	3.56	545*
Standard 1st	1.85	363	2.77	545*	3.23	636	4.19	823
Step-Down 3rd	2.16	240	3.24	360	3.78	420	4.90	545*
Standard 2nd	2.37	363	3.56	545*	4.15	636	5.38	823
Step-Up 1st	2.76	543*	4.14	815	4.83	951	6.26	1,231
Standard 3rd	3.27	363	4.90	545*	5.72	636	7.40	823
Step-Up 2nd	3.55	543*	5.32	815	6.21	951	8.04	1,231
Step-Down 4th	4.49	240	6.74	360	7.88	420	10.34	545*
Step-Up 3rd	4.88	543*	7.32	815	8.54	951	11.06	1,231
Standard 4th	6.82	363	10.23	545*	11.93	634	15.47	823
Step-Up 4th	10.19	543*	15.29	815	17.84	951	23.12	1,231
Step-Down Reverse	2.00	240	3.00	360	3.40	420	4.55	545*
Standard Reverse	3.03	363	4.55	545*	5.31	636	6.88	823
Step-Up Reverse	4.52	543*	6.80	815	7.67	951	10.27	1,231

*ASAE standard PTO speed for PTO tools.
**Full-throttle speeds shown are at an engine speed of 2269 RPM, which is well within the adjustable range of the governor. Engine speed as low as 2,190 puts the "Step-Down" PTO speed within the ASAE standard range of 526 to 546 RPM.

Above and below
This is it, the muscle of V-8 power tucked neatly into the space normally occupied by its little brother, the four-cylinder "L" flathead engine. Big brother's appearance is impressive. Not only that, its deep, throaty growl sounds powerful to the ears. Looks aren't deceiving in this case, either, because the V-8 conversion was easily the brawniest engine to be put to work in an N-Series tractor.

step-up unit offered three ranges, standard, low range, and high range.

Sherman transmissions were available for each of the N-Series tractors. Note the accompanying chart, which shows ground speed and PTO rpm at specific engine rpms.

The need for a broader gear range on the N-Series tractors and success of the Sherman led other companies, such as Hupp, Park, and Howard to offer similar units.

More Powerful Engine Conversions

Maybe it was everything that transpired during World War II , because during the late 1940s Americans were smitten with the notion that bigger is better. Other tractor manufactures such as Case and International Harvester were offering farmers varying tractor models, always with increasing horsepower and tractor weight.

Farm machinery was cutting a wider swath both in tillage machines and PTO equipment. Ford Motor Company, however, got caught making the same mistake with its tractor line—or lack thereof—as it did decades before with its famed Model T. While other manufactories were giving the farmer a wide choice of tractor sizes, Ford still only provided the same number of choices in tractors it always had: one.

The solitary advantage the Ford tractor had going for it was the three-point hydraulic system and matching line of mounted equipment that

Huesinkveld had to design special features to accommodate the standard three-point lift arms when he moved the gas tank rearward to the seat area. The challenge was met with this setup.

many farmers already owned. About this time, at least four people believed it would be cheaper to replace the four-cylinder engines of their Fords than to replace the entire tractor with another make. Two of these innovators were the Funk twins, Joe and Howard, owners of Funk Aircraft Company, Coffeyville, Kansas.

In 1948, the Funk brothers developed and marketed a conversion kit that allowed an owner to drop a six-cylinder Ford flathead under the gray hood of the N tractor. This conversion almost doubled cubic inch displacement, boosting it from 119.7 to a husky 226 cubic inches. About 5,000 to 10,000 of these kits were sold.

The kit also lengthened the tractor's wheelbase by 8 inches and raised the hood 5 inches to accommodate the needed larger radiator. As a final touch, a cast-aluminum supplement to the hood was added just in front of the instrument panel.

The conversion kit, sans engine, cost roughly $250. Most changeovers could be accomplished in one good, long day. The resulting tractor was considerably cheaper than buying a new tractor. However, the operator was well-advised to remember that the transmission and

A 1950 8N V-8 conversion hand-fabricated in 1949 by Delbert Huesinkveld, Springfield, South Dakota, who now lives in Sioux Center, Iowa. Huesinkveld was able to retain the classic lines of the Ford 8N by moving the gas tank rearward to the seat area. This allowed enough clearance so there was no need to raise the hood as with the later Funk conversion kit. However, the hood did require widening. This work was custom-done by a Ford dealership in Yankton, South Dakota. Huesinkveld completely restored the tractor after repurchasing it in 1990.

An aftermarket dampener is mounted on the steering wheel of an 8N tractor. Anyone who's ever driven a tractor hour after hour in the field can appreciate this relatively inexpensive yet highly useful device. If it only saves one busted knuckle, it's worth the price.

A nicely restored 8N V-8 that's been a crowd-pleaser at every show to which it's been transported. Everything on the tractor is original except for the rear tires, rims, and wheels. For some reason, though, nobody ever notices the rear wheels when they see the V-8 engine lurking under the hood.

differential were designed for a more anemic four-cylinder power source. Drop in one of these powerful engines—especially the V-8—and the Ford tractor becomes an altogether different animal. The tractor takes on an aura of barely restrained power that is almost dangerous. The feeling is almost the same with either of the six-cylinder conversions, but they don't have the primal growl of the Ford flathead V-8.

You have to wonder if Harry Ferguson ever experienced a Funk conversion. He probably would have considered the engine conversion a form of overkill. One would think that Henry Ford, on the other hand, would have loved the Funk V-8. Between 1927 and 1938, one of Ford's favorite experimental tractors was a row-crop version that sported a V-8 engine.

V-8 conversion was pointed with Ford-New Holland paint: Gray #MIJ-957 and red #MIJ-956.

Another view of the V-8 conversion backlit by the sinking sun.

So while maybe Henry Ford would have loved it, someone in the Ford organization obviously did not. The story goes that Ford tractors began showing up at the dealerships for warranty work on the transmission and differential. The source of the problem was generally considered to be the Funk conversions and more specifically the added horsepower up front for which the Ford "behind" wasn't built.

Early versions of the six-cylinder conversion kit used four-inch channel iron as structural support rails for the engine. Pretty it wasn't. Later, a cast-iron pan was introduced that eliminated the ugly iron frame, which was a blight on the tractor's belly.

Delbert Heusinkveld, Sioux Center, Iowa, and Quinton Nilson, Akron, Iowa, were two other men who admired the Ford 8N but wished it had more horses under the harness. Both men went directly to a V-8 solution. This more than quadrupled the horsepower from the 8N's factory 22 horsepower to an impressive 100 horsepower.

Huesinkveld, with the help of a brother and cousin, hand-built his first V-8 conversion during the winter of 1949–1950.

At the same time, Quinton Nilson was converting his own 8N to V-8 power. Neither man was aware of the other's conversion efforts. Nilson entered his V-8 in the national terracing competi-

Another 8N Funk conversion. The dual stacks are a treat to the ears and make the tractor look like it means business—hearty pulling business.

tion. He won the event in convincing style over a field of bigger factory-built tractors from all major ag equipment manufacturers.

After meeting Quinton and seeing the results of this V-8, Heuinkveld loaded his V-8 conversion onto a trailer and invited Quinton to accompany him to the Funk factory in Kansas. After a few tests in the field and some market research, the Funk company agreed to offer a kit to convert the N tractor to V-8 engine power. About 225 of these V-8 conversions were eventually sold. The engine cost $250 in 1949.

While the Funk conversion was getting up and running with the V-8, Heuinkveld and crew

hand-built six other V-8 conversions. Their efforts differ from the standard Funk V-8 conversion on two points.

First, the hoods were hand-altered at the Ford dealership in Yankton, South Dakota. This included widening, while retaining the classic lines of the Ford N hood. Because Heuinkveld moved the gas tank to the rear and incorporated it into a wide

Right
Squint hard and you can almost visualize how this six-cylinder flathead Funk conversion, awaiting its turn for restoration, will look within a few months.

The Funk Aircraft Company's cast-aluminum cowling shows the Funk name, model AN, and the number 5116. The serial number is absent from most of the conversions, though. The company suffered a major fire that caused loss of all records during the years that the conversion kits were sold. This loss of records possibly accounts for the lack of serial numbers on many kits produced and sold after the fire.

A round plate installed under the steering wheel nut shows the different combination of gears and speeds available with the Sherman transmission. The plate bears the Sherman name; restorers assume it came with the Sherman transmission.

bench seat, there was no need to ever raise the hood. The result is a tractor that's aesthetically stunning. Heuinkveld has accounted for the location of five of these seven hand-built units. Somewhere out there are two of these babies. Locating one might just be better than winning the lottery.

An overhead valve six-cylinder was later added to the conversion kit line. These are extremely rare. Only about 20 to 30 were built and sold.

You can still step up to V-8 power today thanks to a newly manufactured conversion kit available from R. L. Stauffer, Inc., Portland, Indiana. Check the Appendix for the address.

A Talk with Joe Funk and Bernard Wade

Today, the Funk brothers' conversion kits for the Ford N-Series tractors are enjoying a high degree of interest among collectors and restorers—that's a conservative way of saying that they're extremely hot items and becoming even more so.

With that in mind, here's a closer look at what led up to this popularity and why the conversions became so widespread originally and why there's now a resurgence of ownership.

One of the two Funk brothers and the company's former plant manager and president are still

If you can't locate an original Funk V-8 conversion for restoration you can make your own with these new kit parts. The kit provides parts that are identical to the parts originally used in Delbert Heusinkveld's first hand-built V-8s. For more information see the parts and service section in the appendix.

The Sherman transmission shift lever on this 8N indicates this is a step-up, step-down combination transmission.

101

This left side shot of the Funk six-cylinder overhead valve engine shows the special treatment and care given by owner and restorer Johnny Grist, Maple Hill, Kansas. His experience is typical; several parts were missing when he first acquired the tractor. By investing time in careful research, however, he was able to hand-make a number of needed vital parts—including the carburetor linkage, governor mounting bracket, governor cross-shaft, and air cleaner attachment to the top of the carburetor.

living. Keep in mind, though, that they point this out concerning their Funk conversion kit for the N-Series Ford tractor: "We had a plant fire in October 1954 that destroyed virtually all of our records. And remember, we're trying to recall something about events that happened almost 50 years ago too."

If that answer seems vague, you also need to appreciate that the Funk Aircraft Company manufactured many different kinds of products—ranging from aircraft to tractor transmissions—at its Coffeyville, Kansas, location. The firm employed up to 1,400 people at any one time.

As this book's printing, Joe Funk is an active 86 years old. His twin brother, Howard, died in 1995. Bernard Wade, a plant manager who also served at one time as company president, is still golfing at age 81.

Joe was born 30 minutes before Howard in 1910. Their father was a successful businessman with a chain of five grocery stores. The Funk Aircraft Company, which manufactured the Funk

conversion kit, was founded by the Funk twins at Akron, Ohio.

Perhaps not too surprising, their lives paralleled those of Henry Ford and Harry Ferguson to a remarkable degree. They too shared a strong interest in automobiles, airplanes, tractors, and just about anything else mechanical. Students the Funks were not, though. For example, both boys required ten years to finish eight years of elementary school. However, they each eventually completed a year of college. There was never any argument that their interest was slanted toward the mechanical, not the academic.

While the twins were still teenagers, they rebuilt their first automobile. Coincidental or not, it was a wrecked Model T Ford touring car that their father gave them to fix up.

During World War I and into the 1930s, Akron, Ohio, was a busy place for blimp and dirigible airships. These lighter-than-air aircraft were constantly in the air around the city. Perhaps it

The starter housing on the overhead valve six-cylinder engine shows the Funk name and the company model designation "AN." The "55" is thought to be either a casting number or a part number.

was only natural that the Funk boys were bitten by the flying bug. By age 15 they had scraped together enough money to pay for their first plane ride.

Joe and Howard Funk's relationship with Ford Motor Company dates back to 1937 or 1938 when they modified a Model T engine to power the aircraft they had designed and built. The engine was inverted and mounted backward compared to the usual automobile position, however.

Next page
Johnny Grist's restored six-cylinder overhead valve Funk conversion appears much bigger than a classic N-Series tractor—because it really is a bigger tractor. The conversion kit stretches the wheelbase 9 inches, raises the hood approximately 5 inches, and adds a couple of hundred pounds to the weight of the unit. It's a lot more tractor in both looks and performance.

The Funk name is clearly visible on the front of this cast-iron oil pan for their overhead valve six-cylinder conversion. The cast-iron pan of this later kit provided enough structural strength to eliminate the 4-inch channel iron supports of the earlier kits. Some of the later six-cylinder flat-head conversion kits also featured the cast iron pan.

Because the Funk conversion kits required a larger radiator and additional room above the engine for the gas tank, the hood was raised and moved forward the 9 inches required by the adapter. The cast-aluminum rear hood, as it's called in the company's brochure, was provided to accommodate this modification. This one clearly shows the company name and model number, although it lacks the serial number found on some. According to the Funk sales literature, the AN is their designation for the overhead valve six-cylinder engine.

The Funks inverted the engine to get the prop further off the ground. This in turn enabled them to design a landing gear that didn't require the plane's fuselage to be so high off the ground. Then they reversed the engine in order to mount the propeller where the flywheel would normally be positioned.

Bernard Wade was an early member of the Funk team, because the Funk twins hired him while he was still in high school. He spent his entire working career with the Funk Aircraft Company.

In aviation circles, Clarence Chamberlain, Walter Beech, Amelia Earhart, and Clyde Cessna were some of the big names with whom they rubbed shoulders. And, although their venture into aircraft manufacturing wasn't a monetary success story, the Funks did rack up some significant triumphs.

For instance, the Funks designed the first two-place dual-control glider. They were also the first to launch a glider by towing it with an automobile.

They established an unofficial maximum glider climb record of 2,500 feet per minute for two minutes.

In 1937, their first aircraft was accepted by the U.S. Government's famous "$700 Airplane Program." It met more of the government standards than any other of the entries.

At the time, they were one of only four airplane manufacturers to have both their engine design and air frame design certified by the government.

When it became necessary for glider pilots to be licensed, Joe's license was issued to him, at age 20, in August 1931. It was signed by Orville Wright, the first ever pilot.

The Funk brothers successfully designed and built the first fully tunneled cooling system for aircraft, civilian or military, using liquid coolant engines.

During their up-and-down aircraft manufacturing career they built 365 airplanes. More than half of them, approximately 200, are still flying decades later. This is one of the highest survival rates of any contemporary aircraft built in significant production figures.

A combination of events caused the Funk brothers to cease their efforts with aviation in 1947. These

If you're going to produce a show tractor, you may as well go all out as Johnny Grist did with his 8N six-cylinder overhead valve Funk conversion. The chrome accents attract attention at shows as honey draws flies. Although he likes to keep his exact formula a mystery, Grist says the paint he uses is DuPont Imron and Centari.

reasons included the war years when all aircraft parts were considered essential to the war effort and civilian manufacturing was stopped, funding difficulties, and in post-war years the overabundance of surplus military aircraft that were released to the civilian markets.

In 1978, 31 years after the last airplane rolled out of their factory, the Smithsonian Institute of Aviation recognized the brothers as "American Aviation Pioneers."

Henry Ford and Harry Ferguson were much alike, both being determined, inventive, intuitive, and born with a love for machinery. The Funk twins, although a little later to come on the scene, shared these same characteristics. This, no doubt, helped them accomplish some notable achievements that impacted the Ford N-Series tractors.

The relationship with Ford was at times a bumpy one, according to Joe Funk. But, it's ongoing and alive yet today. For example, the Funk Manufacturing Company, Coffeyville, Kansas, still manufactures parts for Ford-New Holland tractors— even though the company is now a subsidiary of Deere & Company.

Perhaps it was Joe Funk's intuition, or maybe just plain wisdom, that led him in 1946 to pursue another direction for the company.

This concerned development of gear reduction units and flywheel housings for stationary power plants used in oil field industry and irrigation applications. This step eventually led to an initial relationship with Ford, because the engines they utilized were Ford Motor Company's four-cylinder industrial engines.

Then one of Funk's salesman met Ollie Glover, a Ford dealer in central Illinois. Glover was experimenting with installing six-cylinder engines in used Ford N-Series tractors that needed overhauls of their original four-cylinder engines.

The engineering ability of the Funk brothers took this concept and transformed the conversion into a highly marketable and popular product for the Funk Aircraft Company. The Funk conversion kits were sold through Ford dealerships.

The kit they provided didn't include the engine, however. The tractor owner had to purchase the engine from the Ford Motor Company's industri-

This V-8 conversion is striking—and all new. The kit Ron Stauffer, Portland, Indiana, used to convert his 1950 8N is constructed from the same specifications as the original V-8 kit that Delbert Huesinkveld designed in 1949. For availability of these kits see the appendix. This tractor is painted in Ford-New Holland red #MIJ-956 and Ford-New Holland gray #MIJ-957.

al engine division through his Ford dealer. Almost all conversion kits were installed by the Ford dealerships.

Quite soon, the Funks were doing such a large volume of business with Ford Motor Company that Joe would fly to Detroit to spend one week a month at the Ford plant. Everything was going along just dandy.

Then on one of these trips Joe was taken to the Ford boardroom and threatened with a lawsuit over the Funk conversion kits. Ford was convinced that the large six-cylinder engines were the cause of a rash of N-Series differential gear failures. These gears were being turned in as defective to be covered by Ford warranty, and so costing the company money.

However, a further investigation proved the root of the problem was at the Ford production line. Ford, unknowingly, was installing ring gears and pinion gears that hadn't been properly heat-treated. Talk of a lawsuit was dropped, and Funk Aircraft Company continued with production of its popular conversion kits.

Because of the plant fire in 1954 that destroyed all company records, just how many conversion kits were manufactured and sold may never be exactly established.

Yet both Joe Funk and Bernard Wade are confident that the number of flat-head six-cylinder conversion kits they sold was in the range of 5,000 to 10,000, although probably closer to 5,000 than 10,000. Both the V-8 and overhead valve six-cylinder sales were minuscule in numbers by contrast, or "not very many," according to Funk and Wade.

The sales territory for the Funk conversion kits was divided by the Mississippi River. Sales east of the river were dealt with by Ford dealer Ollie Glover. Those west of the river were handled by the Funk factory's sales force.

Just when the cast-iron crankcase oil pan was introduced is uncertain. The castings were done by the Acme Foundry of Coffeyville, Kansas. It's thought that more conversion kits were made with the four-inch channel-iron rail than with the cast-iron pan.

The introduction of the Jubilee Ford in 1953 effectively killed sales of the conversion kits. But, up until that time the Funk conversion kits made the Ford N-Series tractor one of, if not the most, powerful wheel-type tractor available. They were as popular in the tractor pulls of that era as they are with the collectors and restorers of today.

Owners of these tractors enjoyed much respect in their neighborhoods. There's still many a story circulating concerning the prowess of the combination of an N-Series tractor and Funk conversion.

It seems many of these stories involve bets of considerable amounts of money, too. These stories seem to grow with every telling, in which, naturally, the Fords equipped with the Funk conversion kits always won.

Joe Funk relates the tale of a farmer who had a field of Lespedea that over several seasons had become quite mature with a root system that made plowing impossible with the farmer's tractor. He then had the brainstorm that this might be a challenge to whet the tractor pullers' appetites.

So, the farmer decided to make it sporting, meanwhile maybe getting his tough field at last plowed. Word soon got around that this farmer would place a $100 bill somewhere ahead of a tractor. If your tractor had the muscle and could plow to the bill it was all yours.

Farmer after farmer tried with their favorite tractors and plows. But, nobody took home the bill with Ben Franklin's face on it. One day, though, a farmer with an N-Series tractor *a la* Funk conversion showed up to give it a try.

The little tractor was laughed at and its owner was ridiculed, because he had the audacity to even drive into a field where far bigger and mightier tractors had struggled in vain to surge as far as the $100 bill.

Not wanting to leave without at least giving it a try, though, he bravely dropped his plow—and proceeded to plow right over the elusive $100 bill! And, he just kept going, too, not stopping until he had turned the entire Lespedea field black.

This V-8 conversion rear hood was hand-built to dress out a 1950 8N conversion project. It has pleasing lines, although it's somewhat different from the Funk conversion rear hood.

The shift lever on this auxiliary transmission is in the same location as the Hupp but is shorter than the Hupp. Restorers can't agree on the manufacturer, but several think it's mostly likely a Park auxiliary transmission.

Seven

Painting and Restoration Tips

Whats the gravest sin you can commit when restoring an N-Series tractor? "Paint it the wrong color" is the most often heard and plaintive reply by collectors and restorers.

The painting itself is a relative easy step compared to all the preparation work that's required, however. And even before the preparation work you need to reach a decision: Do you do it yourself, farm out the job to the professionals, or do a combination of both? If you're a die-hard do-it-your-selfer, that's great. Depending on your patience and ability, restoration of an N-Series tractor can be both a highly rewarding and satisfying experience. However, don't expect it to be a weekend project.

Before you begin, you need to set some objectives. It's one thing if all you're looking for is a nice gray or gray-and-red tractor with which you can efficiently mow the grass and brush. It's an entirely different ball game if you desire a showroom condition tractor—that end result requires a combination of extra time and money. More and more, serious collectors are opting for a top-end restoration job; and color is always the primary consideration.

Tractor restoration hasn't reached the high degree of detail as automobile restoring as yet. Note, though, that the trend is to be as faithful as possible to the original equipment of the model being finished.

Left
Chester Todd's 1950 8N is picture pretty and textbook perfect for 8N originality, except for the headlights and bumber. Both are aftermarket items

Look closely and you'll see that this early sign has several distinctive features. First, it uses green—which is a highly unusual color for Ford Motor Company advertisements of any era. It has the Ford Motor Company signature in the lower left-hand corner, though, and is made of sturdy porcelain just like your kitchen sink.

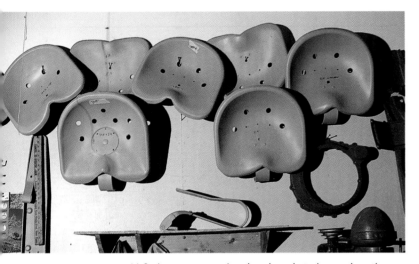

Any paint job is only as good as the prep work that precedes it. Without question, the hardest part of paint preparation is removing some or all of the old paint. This is mandatory for even a reasonable restoration job.

For eventual "parade tractor" results, removal of all parts such as fenders, hood, tires, and rims is a must. The route to successful repair and painting is removal of any items that can be taken off the tractor. Also, either remove or carefully mask off original unpainted parts such as belts and wiring.

N-Series seats are primed and ready to be used on the next needy tractor restoration project. Collecting and restoring the N-Series tractor is becoming so popular that owning any original parts for the tractor is like earning interest on money in the bank.

Below
This original weather cover fits nicely on a war model 2N. Certainly less costly than a new machine shed, the cover keeps the rain, snow, and damaging rays of the sun from reaching the tractor during the times when it's not working in the field.

A new air filter decal adds the finishing touch to a restoration job. This air filter decal was one of three that appeared originally on the production 9N and 2N. The other two were positioned on the oil filter.

Although they look original at a distance, and even when squinting close-up, these decals on the oil filter are reproductions that a restorer purchased.

Gray should be gray with no red over spray or vice versa. Tires don't get paint, not even a little, bitty bit. Period! Radiators are one color only: black.

Liquid paint strippers on the market require no special or expensive equipment to use. A pair of rubber gloves, a putty knife, steel wool, and a truckload of elbow grease—not to mention an abundance of patience—will help you get the job done. Unfortunately, experience leads to the rule of thumb that the more effective the stripper, the less environmentally palatable it is.

For the sheet metal, products such as Klean-Strip's Aircraft Stripper are available. Caution: Read and then always follow the manufacturer's instructions.

The best system for stripping castings such as engine block, transmission, differential, rims, hubs, and front axle is sandblasting. Actually, sandblasting has become an obsolete or generic term that's a holdover from the days when real sand was used. The Environmental Protection Agency (EPA) now outlaws this practice. Plastic beads, called media blasting, and a carbon derivative, called "Black Beauty," are a couple of products used in place of sand today.

Unless you have a well-equipped shop and lots of experience, removing the paint is a task perhaps best left to the professionals who specialize in paint removal. Your cost will be several hundred dollars but is much less expense than purchasing all the equipment necessary to do it yourself. Sandblasting, now more properly known as media blasting, requires a large capacity air compressor, a good quality blasting outfit, and protection gear for the operator. The price tag for such equipment can run into the thousands of dollars.

Indoor blasting requires adequate space and creates a mess. If you try to work outside, wind and

This safety decal is located on the differential housing of all the 8N tractors.

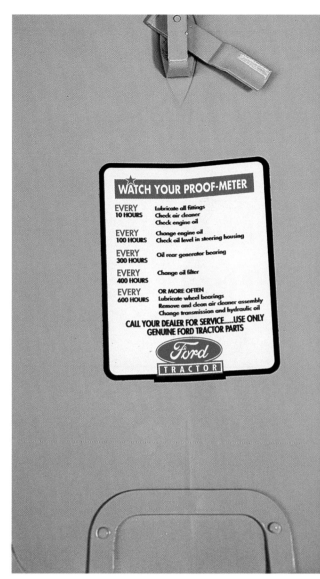

"Proofmeter" decal on the bottom of the hinged battery cover appeared in 1951 with the introduction of the pace-setting, helpful "Proofmeter" on the 8N tractors.

weather can stop or delay your work. Suggestion: Ask those who have had experience removing paint for advice and guidance if you decide to tackle paint removal yourself.

Blasting around the engine requires that all openings to the internal parts be carefully closed off. This ensures that no foreign particles will find their way into the internal parts of your engine.

Flaws in the metal work and any repairs that are needed elsewhere become quite apparent when your tractor and its parts stand before you naked to your gaze. Now is the time to make any necessary repairs.

Don't let the bare metal you expose sit around for too long unprotected, however. Once rust, corrosion, or other contaminates go to work on the raw metal, you'll have additional work to do before you can continue with painting. Immediately priming the metal is your next important step.

Repair any stress fractures in the sheet metal work now. Fill with Bondo dents and dings that you can't pop out. Then dress out smoothly either by hand or by using a power grinder.

Now is also an opportune time to replace any seals, gaskets, or rubber grommets that are missing or worn out. There are always sure to be a few of these that need replacing.

This isn't the time for an engine major overhaul work, however. Any of that work should be completed before you reach this stage.

Note: If you're lucky enough to have one of the original aluminum hoods, grills, side panels, or dashes, take special care when sandblasting, welding, or applying chemicals so nothing has the opportunity to attack the aluminum. Most restorers are polishing these aluminum parts rather than painting over them. Painting over aluminum requires a special primer before painting. Check with your paint supplier for suggestions if you decide to go the paint route. A product that will help you keep aluminum looking good is Everbright. Follow the product instructions.

Decide which brand of paint and primer you're going to use at the same time. That way, the primer will be compatible with the paint for optimum beauty and protection. A good primer is an excellent insurance plan for your restoration. Don't cut any corners here while experiencing an adrenaline rush to get the paint on and see your tractor fin-

An original decal located on the battery cover. Although most battery covers were eventually lost or discarded by owners, they served an important purpose and if at all possible should be part of any original restoration attempt. Directly under this cover is the battery, which makes filling the gas tank dangerous if gas is inadvertently spilled on the battery.

ished. Before actually applying paint, make sure you've sanded the primer and reprimed as needed.

Of course, you'll want to live to enjoy your tractor so follow all recommendations by manufacturers concerning safety procedures and required safety gear. Just because you own a respirator don't assume it's rated for the material you're using. Atomized chemicals from the over spray, the vapor, and even contact with your skin can be extremely hazardous to your health. Don't fail to neglect the environment either. Always dispose of thinners and cleaning materials in accordance with EPA guidelines.

Primers

If your tractor's paint is reasonably good and tight, you may decide not to strip off all the old paint. Use a wax and grease remover before you do any sanding of the old paint. Sanding without this step will grind in any grease or wax that's on the original finish. After you've removed grease and wax, proceed with filling or repairing any stress cracks or scratches.

The primer is the base coat that acts as a bonder to the metal and provides a compatible surface for the final paint. All too often a visit to an automotive paint store will confuse all but the seasoned painter.

Before proceeding further, determine if your tractor's existing paint is lacquer or enamel. To determine this, rub a small area in an inconspicuous spot with lacquer thinner. If the thinner dissolves, the paint is a lacquer finish. Otherwise, it's enamel.

While you can spray enamel over existing lacquer, applying lacquer over enamel can be a problem if the enamel isn't totally cured. And, who knows about this? So, it's safest to always start with a primer-sealer.

Primer-sealers and adhesion promoters seal the new paint from the old layer you're painting over. This ensures against any chemical reaction between the old and new finish and the new paint soaking through into the old paint, causing the color to fade and dull.

Primer-surfacers have a high solids content and will cover minor flaws and scratches. A couple of light coats allowed to thoroughly dry and then wet-sanded will provide you with a smooth surface for painting.

The relatively new, two-part etching primers are a good choice if you've completely stripped the

Another example of cracked side panels. Note that the method of attachment doesn't use the through bolts on the bottom of the panel that later N-Series models employed.

old paint down to bare metal. This product combines the qualities of primer-surfacer and primer-sealer into one. It's also extremely good at retarding corrosion and in bonding well to cast-iron.

Paints

You have three choices: lacquer, enamel, or urethane.

Acrylic lacquer has a liquid plastic binder that provides a hard, durable finish. One distinct advantage is quick drying, almost instantaneously, in fact. This makes a good finish possible without having to resort to a dust-free spray booth. However, you must buff a lacquer in order to achieve a good luster.

On the downside, lacquers are prone to cracking if you apply too many coats without proper drying time between coats. Lacquer also doesn't hold up well to chemicals and fuel spills.

Acrylic enamel gives a tough, highly durable, and weather-resistant finish. It dries more quickly than straight enamel, resists scratches, and has a high-gloss finish.

Disadvantages are that proper dust control is necessary and drying time is much longer than for lacquer. Also, acrylic enamel seems to have an almost magnetic attraction for dust particles and insects and often requires color sanding and polishing to bring out a high luster.

Urethane is part of the enamel family that provides both a rich luster and relatively fast drying time. Urethane is tougher than acrylic enamel. The paint is pricey, as much as 30 percent higher, however, and requires a higher grade of user protection against toxic ingredients. Manufacturers recommend a fresh air mask, complete paint suit, and rubber gloves when handling this product. If this is the paint you choose and if you apply it properly, you won't have to worry about your tractor's finish for a long, long time.

Paint Colors

Battleship gray and forest gray are a couple of names given to the gray color of the 9N and 2N tractors. There's a theory that Ford used the same color of gray as the Navy used on its ships in order to take advantage of the cost effectiveness of a paint produced in such vast quantities. Regardless, Henry Ford's record of forcing suppliers to provide material at the lowest possible prices, sometimes even at cost, is the more likely answer. Ford simply bought paint where it could be purchased at the lowest price.

Even knowing the paint manufacturer and its formula may not be the solution to the color dilemma—which is one of the most common dilemmas first-time restorers encounter. First, minute differ-

It's kind of like finding a gold nugget. This still-new oil filter was located at a Ford dealership. Its paint and decal were as pristine as the day it was shipped from the factory, and it had never been out of the box much less seen time on a tractor. As such, wouldn't it be a really good item to use as a paint color sample? By the way, this same oil filter will fit any N-Series tractor.

ences occur within each batch of paint. Second, the ingredients of 50 years ago may not be available or even legal today.

If you're a purist, don't become discouraged if it's neither feasible nor practical to paint your tractor with the same paint that originally came off the assembly line. At your local Ford-New Holland dealership, they don't even list a paint parts number specifically for the 9N or 2N. Just where does that leave you? With a lot of good options, actually, because paints today are far superior to the original finishes. Thanks to computer color matching and mixing, you have virtually numerically endless shades of color from which to choose in any of several types of paint.

The best advice on choosing your paint color is to make a trip to a paint supplier such as Ditzler, DuPont, or Sherwin-Williams. Take a color sample and get the advice of these professionals. Choose a part from your tractor that's been protected and that exhibits as close to original color as possible.

Hoods, grills, and rims await their turn in the paint finish booth. Notice that because they've been primed, it's all right to let them wait a while before painting. Caution: Always prime any bare metal once it's been stripped of its protective original paint.

A new paint job of the engine, transmission, and differential on a 1953 Ford Jubilee dries in the paint booth.

The store can probably do a good job of matching the paint color either by use of a computer or through professional expertise. Or visit restorers whose tractors you admire; they'll probably be flattered and share their expertise with you.

Naturally, if you're prone to do things your own way and appreciate the custom touch, just go wild. After all, it is your tractor.

Here are some Ford tractor paint colors used by restorers whose tractors are shown in the photographs in this book.

Model 9N and 2N Colors
1. Martin-Senour Paint #6019 Ford-Ferguson gray sold at NAPA Auto-Tractor Supply Houses
2. NAPA #991 21200 gray

3. Tisco #TP230 gray
4. Cote-All Tool Gray #AZ-0405, manufactured by Diamond Vogel Paints, Inc., Orange City, Iowa
5. NAPA #99L3732
6. Black: radiators should be painted with a heat-dispensing paint used by most radiator shops.

Model 8N Colors
1. Ford-New Holland Gray, #M1J-957
2. Ford-New Holland Red, #M1J-956
3. NAPA Ford Red, #7849
4. NAPA #99L-11573, 8N Red
5. NAPA #99L-4338, 8N Gray
6. Acme Paint #3-1750, 8N Gray
7. Acme Paint #3-2822, 8N Red
8. Tisco #240, 8N Gray
9. Tisco #TP110, 8N Red
10. Diamond Vogel Industrial Red, #141959
11. Black: radiators should be painted with a heat-dispensing paint used by most radiator shops. If you choose to paint the starter and generator black, use a semi-gloss engine paint.

Bolts

Over the years, many of the original bolts used to attach the dash have been replaced with a variety of substitutes. Having all these bolts the same is a big plus in looks. Even better, of course, would be having original bolts.

If obtaining original bolts is impossible, check out one of the suppliers that provide aftermarket bolts of the original design. These bolts aren't expensive and can make your tractor even more attractive. Ditto the bolts that attach the air cleaner louvers. Also, see that the hood attachment bolts on the side panels are matched and look original. All of these bolts were originally plated and unpainted.

The 8N lug bolt situation is enough to bring on a migraine headache. Different restorers are adamant about the paint on them or lack thereof. The owner's manual clearly shows the lugs nuts on the front and rear axle to be red. Nevertheless, a Ford Motor Company photograph of an early production 8N tractor shows no paint on these nuts and bolts.

The probable explanation is that early units were unpainted, but that later the decision was made to paint these nuts and bolts red. This is a clear issue where restorer preference is the rule. However, to add to the dilemma, a restorer with years of experience insists that the tractor he bought new in 1950 arrived at his farm with the lug nuts painted red but with the bolts plated and unpainted. Pain reliever, anyone?

Rims can prove about as tough to pin down—although initially they appear simple. The rims were zinc-plated on all production tractors from 1939 to 1952. That holds until you examine a one-piece rim that has no plating. Scratching and picking at the rim, believing it to be so badly weathered that most of the plating is gone, proves otherwise, because no evidence of plating shows up.

It's owner's choice and this tractor looks mighty good. But if you're striving for originality, leaving the throttle lever and the steering wheel acorn nut unpainted would be preferable. One nice thing about tractor collecting and restoring is that nobody is keeping score—everybody's too busy having fun.

Something you certainly won't see too often: An 8N equipped with Bombardier tread tracks. Both floatation and traction capabilities are reported to be excellent with this arrangement. Not too surprisingly, the tracks were developed in Canada by a snowmobile and aircraft company.

So were the real early rims unplated and painted with the rest of the wheel? Again, this seems to be a production change to plating somewhere after the first early 9Ns went out the door. Some restorers are painting the rims gray, others aluminum, and still others a dull aluminum. A bigger bottle of pain medication?

The *9N-2N-8N Newsletter* (volume 2, number 1, Winter 1987), sheds a little light on the subject of bolts in general, although it doesn't answer the question of color choice. The information is from an interview with Harold L. Brock, a Ford .employee who worked closely with both Henry Ford and Harry Ferguson in developing the design of the original N tractor. Brock states:

Oversize hex heads were used on the 7/16-inch bolt that was heat-treated and plated. And, the other hardware, such as the nut to go with the bolt, was also plated and heat-treated.

A close-up of the Bombardier tread tracks shows the curved metal bars that track over the rear tires. They track nicely when properly mounted and aren't prone to running off the tires.

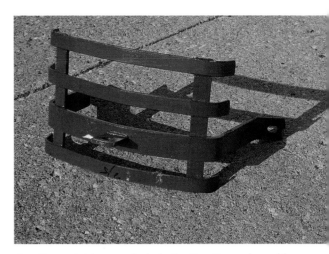

An aftermarket bumper looks both attractive and capable of doing its job. But notice the bar for mounting is straight. The original bumper had a slight curve downward just after the bend for mounting on the axle. A question restorers haven't yet completely resolved: Was the bend down on the original Ford bumper to allow the crank to line up with the crank hole?

The larger hex permitted longer life without rounding off the hex surfaces. All the bolt ends were rounded off, and extended only one-and-one-half threads to prevent catching clothing or injuring the operator.

Decals

The final finishing touch to complete your restored tractor is the outfitting of proper decals. No matter how good a job you do on restoring and painting, your tractor will obviously look like it's missing something important without the decals—the total effect will be one of looking like you quit too soon.

There are two basic types of decals. One is the water transfer type that you soak in water, slip off the backing, and apply to the desired location on your tractor. A Mylar decal, on the other hand, has a peel-off backing similar to that of contact paper. Be sure the decal is aligned properly, because once in good contact with the metal surface it's extremely difficult to redo.

The raised Ford insignia or logo on the hood and fenders of the 8N were originally painted. If you have a steady hand and an artistic flare,

Are you going to use your N-Series tractor for work rather than show? Then it may not be as important to you to display the proper emblems. For a show tractor, however, proper emblems are almost a necessity. Suggestion: Aftermarket emblems are available if your project tractor lacks the right emblems and you can't scrounge any original emblems.

December 19, 1949, dates this 8N tractor operator's manual.

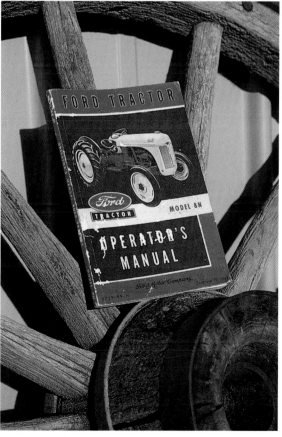

you can hand-letter these. A professional sign painter or artist can probably make an insignia look factory original.

The 9N and 2N have three original decals. Two are located on the oil filter and one is on the air cleaner.

The 8N came with one on the draft control, one safety decal on the rear axle housing, and one under the hood lid that pertained to the "Proofmeter." These decals are in addition to the same three decals that are on the 9N and 2N, two on the oil filter and one on the air cleaner.

Parts Service and Information

The tractor collecting and restoring phenomenon has reached around the world. In almost every part of the United States and in many other countries Ford tractor parts are available from businesses specializing in new and used parts for the N-Series. Even today's Ford-New Holland dealerships carry a line of some new parts. Although it's impossible to list every source, the following resources can provide you with some help.

A high-tech way to get in touch with those who are of like mind and may know of other suppliers is to surf the World Wide Web or Internet via your computer modem. To subscribe to the tractor collector's mailing list, send E-mail to: antique-tractor-request@ co.forsythe.nc.us. A subscription service page is available on the World Wide Web at http://freenet. co.forsyth.nc.us/tractor/atis.html

Hundreds of meets and shows across the country put buyers and sellers together. The *Steam and Gas Show Directory* gives a comprehensive calendar of these events. For a copy, write to Stemgas Publishing Company, P.O. Box 328, Lancaster, PA 17608.

Another rich source of N-Series information is the *N-Newsletter* published by Gerard W. Rinaldi, P.O. Box 235, Chelsea, VT 05038-0235.

Intertec Publishing publishes a book listing U.S. sources of parts and services for antique tractors and restoration. Write to them at P.O. Box 12901, Overland Park, KS 66282-2901.

Parts, Service and Information

Dwight Emstrom
Emstrom Farm Antiques
RR 2, Box 140
Galesburg, IL 61401
Phone 309-342-9075
    Collector, restorer, parts, and equipment

Johnny and Linda Grist
South Topeka Service
4700 S. Topeka Blvd.
Topeka, KS 66609
Phone 913-862-3904
    Collector, restorer, parts, and equipment

Palmer Fossum
Palmer Fossum Fords
10201 E. 100th St.
Northfield, MN 55057
Phone 507-645-8095
    Collector and restorer; Fordson, Ford, and Ferguson parts and service

R. L. Stauffer, Inc.
7780 S. US 27
Portland, Indiana 47371
Phone 219-726-4206 Fax 219-726-2521
    Collector, restorer, 8N conversion kits, "N" Series restoration, parts, and service

Branson Enterprises
7722 Elm Ave
Rockford, IL 61115
Phone 815-633-4262
    Carburetor and magneto sales, service, and parts

Bob Johnson
503 1st Street
Jackson, MN 56143
Phone 507-847-3755
    Complete engine service rebuilding and carburetor, distributor, magneto, and governor rebuilding

Oliver Smith
305 S. 2nd Street
Denton, MD 21629
Phone 410-479-0872 Fax 410-479-0730
    Authentic 8N decals, authentic steering column rubber grommets, and special dome headed bolts for dash to hood

Calyx Corp.
PO Box 53277
Cincinnati, OH 45253
Phone 513-923-1154 Fax 513-923-1154
Wats 1-800-313-5671
   Manufacture and distribution of an exhaust maifold dressing which is for detailing. Handles no tractor parts

Mag-Electro Service
HCR 2, Box 88
Friona, TX 79035
Phone 806-295-3682
   Magneto parts, sales, and service for Ford tractors

Ed Strain, Inc.
6555 44th St. #2006
Pinellas Park, FL 33781
Phone 1-800-266-1623
   Magneto sales and repair

Russel Gibson Tractor and Gas Engine Restoration
202 Shirley, P.O. Box 225
Richland, MO 65556
Phone 573-765-3551
   Tractor and engine repair and painting

Somerset Welding
Box 4055
Athens, ME 04912
Phone 207-654-3332
   All types of repairs and complete restoration

Inga, Inc.
The Brassworks
289 Prado Road
San Luis Obispo, CA 93401
Phone 1-800-342-6759 Fax 805-544-5616
   Rebuild original N-Series radiatiors using a new core installed into existing original radiator. Call for price and delivery time.

Panning Bros. Tractor Parts
Rt. 1, Box 19
Gibson, MN 55335
Phone 507-834-6512 Fax 507-834-9713
Wats 1-800-635-0993
   New, rebuilt, used and aftermarket parts. Free nationwide parts locating service

M. E. Miller Tire Company
17386 State Highway 2
Wauseon, OH 43567
Phone 419-335-7010 Fax 419-335-9881
   For antique tractors: Tires, tubes, wheels, and tire reliners, tire repair materials

Gempler's, Inc.
P. O. Box 270
Mt. Horeb, WI 53572
Phone 1-800-382-8473 Fax 1-800-551-1128
   Front and rear tires, tubes, rims, and wheels for the Ford N-Series tractors. Tire changing and repair equipment, tire paint, and tire chains. Ship nationwide.

Wallace W. Wade Specialty Tires
530 Regal Row, P.O. Box 560906
Dallas, TX 75356-0906
Phone 214-688-0091 Fax 214-634-8465
Wats 1-800-666-TYRE
   Tires for antique tractors, cars, and pickups. Militar tires plus banners and pennants for shows

E-Jay Parts and Service
RR 1, Box 172
Gillespie, IL 62033
Phone 217-839-2064
   New, used, and reproduction parts

Pete's Tractor Salvage, Inc.
Rt. 1, Box 124
Anamoose, ND 58710
Phone 701-465-3274 Fax 701-465-3276
U. S. and Canada Wats 1-800-541-7383
    Used tractor and machinery parts

Surplus Tractor Parts Corp.
3215 Main Ave.
P.O. Box 2125
Fargo, ND 58103
Phone 701-235-7503 Fax 701-280-9328
    New, used, rebuilt tractor parts. Diecast model replicas. Reference books. Catalog available

Minn-Kota
15570 485th Ave.
Milbank, SD 57252
Phone 605-432-4315
    Recovering steering wheels and restoration on torsion springs for Rest-O-Ride seats

Strojney Implement Company
1122 Highway 153 E.
Mosinee, WI 54455
Phone 715-693-4515 Fax 715-953-4515
    New, used, and original replacement parts and equipment for sale or trade

Stevens Tractor
RR 1, Box 32B
Coushatta, LA 71019
Phone 1-800-333-9143 Fax 318-932-9800
    New replacement part for many tractors. Heavy in old Ford tractor parts-9N through 1964. Free catalog

Medina Tractor Sales
6080 Norwalk Rd.
Nedina, OH 44256
Phone 336-725-4951
    Tractor repair, parts, owners and repair manuals

Classic Motorbooks
PO Box 1
729 Prospect Ave.
Osceola, WI 54020
Phone 1-800-826-6600 Fax 715-294-4448
    Large selection of books on tractor restoration.

Diamond Farm Book Publishers
P.O. Box 537
Alexandria, NY 13607
Phone 613-475-1771 Fax 613-475-3748
Wats 1-800-481-1353
 E mail diamond@intarnet.on.ca
    Large selection of agricultural tractor, machinery, and livestock books and videos. Tractor service manuals

Intertec Publishing
PO Box 12901
Overland Park, KS 66212
Phone 1-800-262-1954 Fax 1-800-633-6219
    Tractor repair manuals for all brands, used tractor valuation guide book, and a directory listing over 1800 business nationwide that service or sell tractors or tractor related products.

King's Books
P.O. Box 86
Radnor, OH 43066-0086
Phone 614-595-3332
    Reprint manuals, books on Ford tractors: 8N-9N-2N, Fordson, NAA 601-801, 701-901, and sales brochures. Free catalog for the asking

Clarence L. Goodburn Literature Sales
101 West Main St.
Madelia, MN 56062
Phone 507-642-3281 Fax 507-642-3281
    Sales literature, calendars, magazines, and books on farm tractors and equipment

John Skarstad
Department of Special Collections
Shields Library
University of California
Davis, CA 95616
Phone 916-752-1621
    Largest collection of shop parts manuals in the country.

Bibliography

Baber, John, and George Field. *Harry Ferguson—A Brief History of His Life and Tractors*. Coventry, United Kingdom: Massey-Ferguson Tractors Limited, 1993.

Beach, G. Dale. *It's a Funk!* Terre Haute, Indiana: SunShine House, 1985.

Bryan, Ford R. *The Fords of Dearborn*. Detroit, Michigan: Harlo, 1989.

Farmers in a Changing World. Washington D.C.: U.S. Department of Agriculture, 1940.

Fraser, Colin. *Tractor Pioneer: The Life of Harry Ferguson*. Athens: Ohio University Press, 1973 .

Harry Ferguson—A Tribute. United Kingdom: Royal Norfolk Agriultural Society, 1994.

Intertec Ford Shop Manual. Overland Park, Kansas: Intertec Publishing, 1995. ·

Lacey, Robert. *Ford: The Men and the Machine*. Boston: Little, Brown & Company, 1986.

Leffingwell, Randy. *The American Farm Tractor*. Osceola, WI: Motorbooks International, 1991.

Pripps, Robert N. *Illustrated Ford & Fordson Tractor Buyer's Guide*. Osceola, WI: Motorbooks International, 1994.

Pripps, Robert N. *How to Restore Your Farm Tractor*. Osceola, WI: Motorbooks International, 1992.

Ruddiman, Margaret Ford. "Memories of My Brother, Henry Ford." *Michigan History* (volume 37, number 4, September, 1953).

Sorensen, Charles E. *My Forty Years with Ford*. New York, New York: W.W. Norton & Co., 1956.

Sward, Keith. *The Legend of Henry Ford*. New York: Atheneum, 1968.

Williams, Michael. *Ford & Fordson Tractors*. Alexandria Bay, New York: Farming Press, 1985.

Index